e *Secrets* to
1asterful Meetings

Ignite a Meetings Revolution!

Liss'
Great Level 3!
Wow your groups with it

Michael Wilkinson
CEO, Leadership Strategies, Inc.
Author, *The Secrets of Facilitation*

Foreword by Richard Smith

Leadership **Strategies**
The Facilitation Company

56 Perimeter Center East, Suite 103
Atlanta, Georgia 30346
800.824.2850
www.leadstrat.com

Substantial discounts on bulk quantities are available to corporations, governments, non-profits, and other organizations. For details and discount information, contact Leadership Strategies at 800.824.2850.

Library of Congress Cataloging-in-Publication Data

Wilkinson, Michael, 1957-
The secrets to masterful meetings: ignite a revolution that drives bad meetings out of your organization! /
Michael Wilkinson – 1st ed.

ISBN 0-9722458-0-4

1. Business meetings   2. Group facilitation
3. Conflict management   4. Communication in management
I. Title

Library of Congress Control Number: 2005934747

Manufactured in the United States of America
Cover design by Anna Raley
FIRST EDITION
HB Printing   10 9 8 7 6 5 4 3

Your Meeting Rights

(abbreviated)

I.   **Meeting Notice.**
You have the right to be informed about the purpose, expected products, and proposed agenda for a meeting, verbally or in writing, at least twenty-four hours in advance of the meeting.

II. **Timely Start.**
You have the right to attend meetings that start on time.

III. **Right People.**
You have the right to have all major viewpoints critical to decision-making represented at the meeting.

IV. **Right Information.**
You have the right to have the information necessary to facilitate decision-making available at the meeting.

V.   **Ground Rules.**
You have the right to have agreed upon ground rules respected in the meeting.

VI. **Focused Discussion.**
You have the right for meetings to stay focused on the topic of the meeting.

VII. **Input Opportunity.**
You have the right to have the opportunity to provide input and alternative views before decision-making occurs in the meeting.

VIII. **Meeting Recap.**
You have the right to hear a recap of (a) decisions made during the meeting, (b) actions to be taken, when and by whom, following the meeting, and (c) any outstanding issues to be discussed at a future meeting.

IX. **Timely Completion.**
You have the right to have your time respected by having meetings finish at or before the scheduled end time.

X.   **No Retribution.**
You have the right to exercise *Your Meeting Rights* without fear of retribution or other consequences.

To Sherry, Danielle, and Gabrielle

Table of Contents

Part III. What If?

Part IV. Declare War on Bad Meetings

Acknowledgements

No book is created without the help and support of special people.

To authors Michael Doyle and David Straus, whose breakthrough book, *How to Make Meetings Work!*, paved the way for many of us who have followed, I am grateful.

To my copy editor, Carolyn Weiss at Vork Editing, I thank you for translating my passive to active, eliminating my many comma splices, and making the book readable.

To Cathy Alper, Eileen Dowse, Anita Hope, and Judy Jablon, I say thank you for your critical review of this work. Your insights and suggestions greatly improved the content and flow.

To the team of employees and contractors at Leadership Strategies, I owe a wealth of thanks for the support you continue to provide to me. I especially want to thank Richard Smith and Anna Raley who made direct contributions to the book.

To my two young daughters, Danielle and Gabrielle, I say thank you for your love and for being willing to share your dad with the world.

To Sherry, my cherished partner, thank you, darling, for loving me through this process and for all that you do to make our journey simply incredible.

Finally, I thank our Creator for providing the thoughts, the tools, and the motivation to put the ideas into a form for others to use.

Foreword

Why are so many of the meetings we attend less fruitful than we would like? How often have we heard or thought about that dilemma? I know in my twenty-plus years of business experience as a consultant, an executive with software companies, and now as a leader in a consulting firm, I have wondered why meetings are so often less productive than I know they could and should be. While I believed I knew how to avoid the bad meeting pitfalls, I also knew that I was doing it instinctively. I didn't have a framework for making it repeatable or a process that I could explain to others.

In *The Secrets to Masterful Meetings*, Michael Wilkinson shares the processes Leadership Strategies has been using for over a decade to facilitate effective and efficient meetings for our clients. Effective in that the meetings accomplish the purpose intended. Efficient in that the meeting is timely; the right people attend; the discussion stays focused; participants tackle the issues and make decisions; there is agreement on the results; and follow-up occurs.

When you read *The Secrets to Masterful Meetings*, you will find a practical, no-nonsense approach to transforming meetings. The approach will save hundreds of hours spent in meetings that lack purpose, focus, structure, and leadership.

- ❏ In Part I of the book, Wilkinson challenges leaders to ignite a grassroots revolution focused on eliminating bad meetings inside their organizations. He introduces the concept of granting employees meeting rights that serve as a key catalyst for transforming bad meetings into *Masterful Meetings*.

- ❏ However, granting rights without a framework for executing those rights could result in chaos. So, in Part II, he presents an approach to executing *Masterful Meetings*. From a solid method for planning and executing to a focused approach to closing meetings with tools that hold people accountable, these chapters are full of rich, practical, and easily understood practices that will lead to more productive meetings.

❑ Wilkinson then provides a wealth of "what if?" solutions. What if one person is dominating? What if the discussion drifts from topic to topic? What if a participant consistently speaks negatively about every recommendation that arises? What if there is conflict? What if the leader isn't leading? What if the meeting is virtual? Part III provides solutions for these situations as well as a multitude of others.

❑ In the final chapter, Wilkinson provides a *Master Plan* to transform your meetings. It is a focused, step-by-step approach to bring about a cultural revolution that makes bad meetings unacceptable within your organization. The steps include gaining leadership buy-in and providing the necessary tools as well as measuring progress and rewarding successes. The revolution is designed to raise the bar on the quality of meetings and to drastically reduce the number of bad meetings.

❑ The book is compact and usable. Most concepts are presented in one or two pages. Checklists appear throughout the book for ease of use. The table of contents alone serves as a great reminder of how to run *Masterful Meetings*.

Practical, straight-forward, and right on point.

If your organization is one of the many that suffers from meetings that are not well run, or if you are one of the executives who spends over fifty percent of the work day in meetings, *The Secrets to Masterful Meetings* is for you. Once you have read the book, you may want to **give yourself a gift:** get a copy for everyone whose meetings you attend!

Richard Smith
Director, Training & Facilitation
Leadership Strategies, Inc.

The *Secrets* to Masterful Meetings

Ignite a Meetings Revolution!

Part I.
Ignite a
Revolution

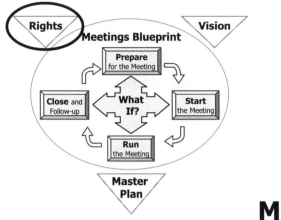

Chapter 1.
Establishing
Meeting Rights

If you are the leader of a team, a department, or an entire organization, ask your people about the meetings they attend. You will likely find that many spend half or more of their time in unproductive, ineffective, dispiriting, and unnecessary meetings.

Bad meetings waste time, consume resources, and wear down people's energy and passion. Still worse, bad meetings often result in bad decisions: decisions which are poorly thought through, void of innovation, and missing the necessary buy-in for success. And yet even worse, we have lowered the bar so far that bad meetings have become the norm. We have accepted them as a necessary evil.

How did we get here? How did we get to the point where we have made bad meetings acceptable? How do otherwise productive-minded people allow the habitual waste of their time by meetings that . . .

- Don't have a purpose.
- Don't stay on topic.
- Don't have key people present.
- Don't engage those who are.
- Don't address conflict.

- Don't reach a decision.
- Don't create results.
- Don't start on time.
- Don't end on time.
- Don't have follow-up actions.

Enough is enough. It is time to ignite a meetings revolution. It is time to make bad meetings unacceptable!

How do you do it? How do you rid your organization of bad meetings? It starts with empowering people with a set of meeting rights and providing meeting leaders with the knowledge and skills to honor those rights. Buckle your seatbelt: the ride is about to get rocky. Let's get started with a fundamental vehicle for transforming meetings.

Your Meeting Rights

What would be the impact on meetings in your organization if one morning, all employees received this e-mail and acted on it?

> We take great pride in our organization's ability to continuously increase the value we provide to our customers and stakeholders. We do this through our relentless drive to improve what we do and how we do it. Unfortunately, bad meetings are undermining this drive for excellence. Bad meetings waste our time, waste our resources, have a negative effect on the passion we have for our work, and, far too often, result in poor decisions.
>
> Meetings are a key vehicle for how we function as an organization, and we must demand a higher value from them. With *Your Meeting Rights*, the Leadership Team is seeking to ignite a meetings revolution. We are asking you and everyone in our organization to help make bad meetings unacceptable. We believe meetings will change if individuals stand up and exercise these rights.
>
> It will be uncomfortable initially, especially when you have to tell a Leadership Team member that he or she is violating one of the meeting rights! But if we stick with the program, we will get past this awkwardness, and the result will be meetings that are more focused, more efficient, and far more effective than what we have today. Help us get there. We invite you and encourage you to exercise these meeting rights.
>
> The Leadership Team

I. **Meeting Notice.**
You have the right to be informed about the purpose, expected products, and proposed agenda for a meeting, verbally or in writing, at least twenty-four hours in advance of the meeting. A full meeting notice includes the following information:

- ❏ Purpose, expected products, and proposed agenda.
- ❏ Location and start and end times.
- ❏ Invited attendees.
- ❏ Recommended items to bring.

You have the right to decline to attend a meeting if your repeated request for this information is not honored without a reasonable cause, unless the meeting is an emergency session or a regular, ongoing meeting for which all attendees know the above information.

II. **Timely Start.**
You have the right to attend meetings that start on time. If, despite your repeated request for the meeting to begin, a meeting does not start within eight minutes of the scheduled start time, you have the right to leave the meeting unless a majority of participants agrees to delay the start.

III. **Right People.**
You have the right to have all major viewpoints critical to decision-making represented at the meeting. If a majority agrees that one or more critical viewpoints are missing and if a reasonable effort is not made to have these viewpoints represented, you have the right to decline to attend future meetings until such an effort is made.

IV. **Right Information.**
You have the right to have the information necessary to facilitate decision-making available at the meeting. If a majority in the meeting agrees that readily accessible information critical for decision-making is not available at the meeting, you have the right to request that the decision be delayed until such information is made available, unless a majority agrees that the consequences of delay overrule the risk of a decision made with inadequate information.

V.   **Ground Rules.**
You have the right to have agreed upon ground rules respected in the meeting. If a ground rule continues to be broken, despite your repeated request that the ground rule be respected, you have the right to leave the meeting.

VI.   **Focused Discussion.**
You have the right for meetings to stay focused on the topic of the meeting. If a meeting continues to spend time on topics not directly related to the agenda despite your repeated attempts to bring the conversation back to the agenda, you have the right to leave the meeting, unless a majority in the meeting agrees to spend time on the unrelated topics.

VII.   **Input Opportunity.**
You have the right to have the opportunity to provide input and alternative views before decision-making occurs in the meeting. Should decision-making or attempts at decision-making occur without the opportunity for input from all meeting participants, you have the right to ask for the suspension of the decision until all participants have had the opportunity to provide input.

VIII.   **Meeting Recap.**
You have the right to hear a recap of (a) decisions made during the meeting, (b) actions to be taken, when and by whom, following the meeting, and (c) any outstanding issues to be discussed at a future meeting. Should a meeting recap not begin at least five minutes before the scheduled end of the meeting, you have the right to request that the recap begin immediately.

IX.   **Timely Completion.**
You have the right to have your time respected by having meetings finish at or before the scheduled end time. Should a meeting continue beyond the scheduled end time despite your reminder, you have the right to leave the meeting, unless a majority of the participants agrees to extend the meeting for a defined period of time.

X.   **No Retribution.**
You have the right to exercise *Your Meeting Rights* without fear of retribution or other consequences. If you believe that this right has been violated, notify your supervisor, meeting coach, or senior team member who will take the appropriate action.

The Masterful Meetings Framework

Imagine the impact if everyone in your organization was granted and exercised *Your Meeting Rights*. These rights were designed to empower meeting participants to make bad meetings unacceptable and help leaders ensure that meetings are effective and productive.

However, granting a provocative list of rights could result in anarchy if you don't provide a vision of something better, a blueprint for creating it, and a process for sustaining it. The *Masterful Meetings Framework* does just this. This book is organized around the four components of the *Masterful Meetings Framework*.

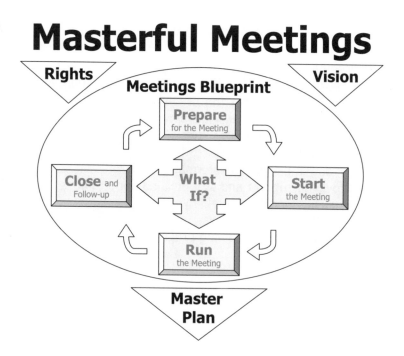

Your Meeting Rights

□ As you have read, Chapter 1 describes the tools for empowering meeting participants to make bad meetings unacceptable.

Masterful Meetings Vision

□ Chapter 2 defines the vision of *Masterful Meetings* and the role meeting leaders and meeting participants play in creating this vision.

Masterful Meetings Blueprint

❑ Chapters 3–7 provide a roadmap for meeting leaders to prepare, start, execute, and close *Masterful Meetings*.

❑ Chapters 8–11 provide a series of "what if" scenarios.
  - What if there is dysfunctional behavior?
  - What if there is disagreement?
  - What if the meeting leader is not leading?
  - What if the meeting is virtual?

The Master Plan

❑ Finally, chapter 12 provides a step-by-step *Master Plan*. While the *Masterful Meetings Blueprint* provides a guide for meeting leaders to run a great meeting, the *Master Plan* provides a guide for organizational leaders to transform all meetings inside the organization.

❑ The *Master Plan* covers key steps for transformation, including:
  - Gaining buy-in from the organization's leaders to implement the *Masterful Meetings Framework.*
  - Establishing a baseline that measures the current effectiveness of meetings.
  - Putting in place a transformation team.
  - Providing support and skill-building opportunities.
  - Implementing accountability.
  - Rewarding successes.
  - Measuring and sustaining progress.

What This Book Will Do For You

This book is designed to help you create a revolution inside your organization. If successful, this revolution will ignite a transformation that creates a culture within your walls that drives out bad meetings.

At the foundation of many successful revolutions are four critical attributes.

Attributes of a Successful Revolution	❑ Wide dissatisfaction with the status quo.
	❑ A commonly held vision of something better.
	❑ A method for engaging every individual to action.
	❑ A collective will to do what is necessary.

Right now, your organization may only have the first attribute: wide dissatisfaction with the way meetings are currently run. This book will help you with the other three.

❑ This book will help you develop a vision of something better.

❑ This book will show you how to engage your people to action.

❑ And it will guide you in creating the collective will to rid your organization of bad meetings.

But most importantly, this book will provide you with a leadership roadmap for igniting the revolution within your organization and for actively and continuously fanning the flames until that fire takes on a life of its own. The result of the revolution will be a permanent transformation in the way meetings are planned and executed.

Whether you are a meeting leader or a meeting participant, you can help ignite a revolution against bad meetings in your organization.

1. Meet with the head of your team, department, or organization to review the meeting rights described in the previous pages. Create a customized version of *Your Meeting Rights* for your organization.

2. Develop a plan for eradicating bad meetings. The *Master Plan* in Chapter 12 provides a starting point.

3. Gain permission to:
   - Distribute the customized version of *Your Meeting Rights*.
   - Post *Your Meeting Rights* in meeting rooms.
   - Exercise *Your Meeting Rights* in meetings.
   - Provide resources and training to meeting leaders and meeting participants on their roles in creating *Masterful Meetings*.

4. In every meeting that **you lead**, use the concepts in this book. Be a role model for *Masterful Meetings*.
   - Use the checklists found at the beginning of the chapters in Part II for preparing, starting, running, and closing meetings.
   - Use the "what if" scenarios in Part III to help you react when disagreements occur or when someone behaves in a dysfunctional way.

5. In every meeting that **you attend** within your organization, exercise *Your Meeting Rights*. Speak up when meetings start late, when the agenda or purpose is not clear, or when the group strays off topic or becomes unfocused.

6. Most importantly:
   - Don't support mediocrity.
   - Don't passively allow your time and energy to be wasted.
   - Don't sit through another bad meeting.
   - Exercise *Your Meeting Rights*!

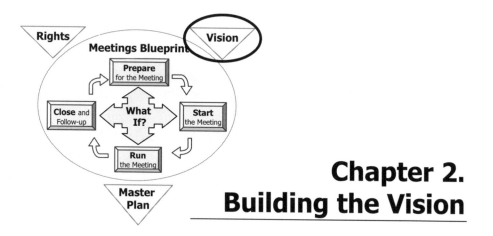

Chapter 2.
Building the Vision

Eliminating bad meetings requires an understanding of the problems that cause them. Participants in hundreds of our workshops at Leadership Strategies over the past decade have repeatedly identified a common set of meeting problems. The diagram on the next page shows these meeting problems and their eight likely root causes. To maintain clarity, the table shows only the one or two primary root causes for each problem.

Root Causes of Bad Meetings

- **Insufficient planning** surrounding the purpose, agenda, participants, timing, and information needed.

- **Lack of commitment** by participants to prepare for the meeting, arrive on time, stay until completion, and give full attention to the meeting topics.

- **Lack of control** by the meeting leader to keep the meeting on track and within time limits while maintaining an appropriate level of detail with balanced, respectful participation.

- **Lack of respect** by meeting participants for each other as evidenced by interrupting one another, side conversations, verbal attacks, and physical attacks.

- **Insufficient follow-up** by not documenting decisions and assigning actions, or not following-up to ensure that assigned actions are completed.

- **Lack of interest and engagement** generated during the meeting that results in low energy and low participation.

- **Inadequate decision-making process** leading to lack of consensus, decisions not being reached, conflict, or conflict-avoidance behaviors.

❏ **A sense of futility** by participants, believing that their efforts won't have an effect, or **a fear of retribution** if they speak up, causing them to not give full, open, and honest dialogue.

Meeting Problems and Root Causes

The Characteristics of Masterful Meetings

Masterful Meeting is the term we use at Leadership Strategies to refer to a vision of what all meetings should be. In summary, a Masterful Meeting can be described as follows:

A *Masterful Meeting* is a well-prepared, well-executed, and results-oriented meeting with a timely start, a decisive close, and a clear follow-up plan.

Masterful Meetings have eighteen specific characteristics that overcome the problems and root causes on the prior page. These characteristics closely align with *Your Meeting Rights* to create the type of meetings to which we believe everyone has the right.

Preparation

1. **Clear Purpose, Products, and Agenda.**
   The meeting leader defines the purpose, products, and agenda that validate the need for a meeting.

2. **Advance Notification.**
   Participants know the purpose, products, proposed agenda, and other key information about the meeting in advance.

3. **Right People—Prepared and Present.**
   The right people are at the meeting. They arrive prepared, they arrive on time, and they stay for the duration.

4. **Right Information.**
   All necessary information is available at the meeting.

Start

5. **Timely Start.**
   The meeting starts on time.

6. **Purpose and Products Reviewed.**
   At the start of the meeting, the meeting leader reviews the meeting purpose and desired products.

7. **Key Issues Identified.**
   Either during the meeting or in advance, all participants have a chance to identify key issues or topics that need to be discussed to achieve the purpose and products.

Masterful Meetings - Characteristics

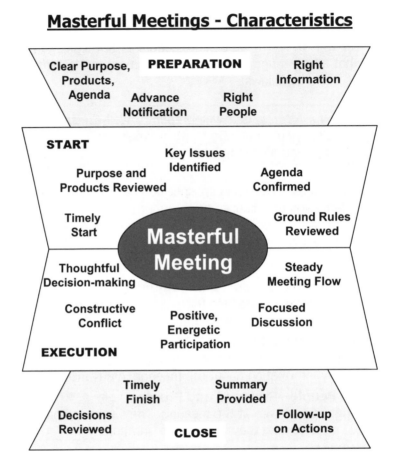

8. **Agenda Confirmed.**
   The meeting leader confirms the agenda and establishes time limits for each item. The leader may choose to adjust the agenda to ensure all key issues are discussed.

9. **Ground Rules Reviewed.**
   The meeting leader reminds the participants of ground rules. Participants honor the ground rules throughout the meeting.

Execution

10. **Steady Meeting Flow.**
    As the meeting flows from one agenda item to the next, the meeting leader reminds the participants of the purpose for each agenda item, how the agenda item fits into the overall meeting

objective, and what the group is being asked to accomplish with the agenda item.

11. **Focused Discussion.**
The discussion remains focused on the topic at hand. A topic is allowed to exceed its allotted time only with the expressed agreement of a majority and with full knowledge of the effect on the remaining agenda items.

12. **Positive, Energetic Participation.**
All participants are actively engaged throughout the meeting. They feel it is safe to speak openly and honestly. People talk and listen with respect. There is energized discussion and debate. No one dominates the discussion.

13. **Constructive Conflict.**
Disagreement is encouraged and conflict is handled by participants asking questions, identifying strengths, defining concerns, and seeking new alternatives that maximize strengths and reduce concerns.

14. **Thoughtful Decision-making.**
Prior to decision-making, appropriate time is given to inviting input, identifying alternatives, and evaluating potential solutions.

Close and Follow-up

15. **Decisions and Actions Reviewed.**
During the meeting, issues that arise that are inappropriate for discussion are deferred to an issues list; decisions made and actions to be taken are documented. Prior to ending the meeting, all issues, decisions, and actions are reviewed, and appropriate action designated.

16. **Timely Finish.**
The meeting ends on time.

17. **Summary Provided.**
Following the meeting, a meeting summary is distributed to all participants. The meeting summary includes issues, decisions, actions, and relevant analysis.

18. **Follow-up on Actions.**
A follow-up process is put in place to ensure all assigned actions are performed.

What Do Masterful Meeting Leaders Do?

Meeting leaders are ultimately responsible for the quality and effectiveness of their meetings. While you will find details on planning, starting, running, and closing meetings in Part II, the list that follows summarizes the role of meeting leaders:

Planning and Preparing

1. Determine the meeting type, purpose, and products.
2. Select participants.
3. Identify probable issues that need to be addressed.
4. Develop the proposed agenda.
5. Select the processes that will be used in executing the agenda, and define the engagement strategies.
6. Hold discussions as needed prior to the meeting.
7. Select the meeting location, and handle other logistics.
8. Prepare and distribute the meeting notice.

Starting Meetings

9. Setup the meeting location, including any parking boards that will be used.
10. Greet people when they arrive.
11. Provide a two-minute warning prior to the start of the meeting.
12. Start the meeting by stating the purpose and products.
13. Ask participants to identify key issues to be discussed.
14. Review the proposed agenda; modify as needed to address the key issues; establish time limits for each item.
15. Remind the participants of the ground rules and parking boards.
16. Make introductions if needed.

Running, Closing, and Following-Up

17. Review prior action items to ensure follow-up.
18. For each agenda item: (FIRST CLASS)
    - **F**ocus the participants by providing an explanation of how the item furthers the meeting's purpose.
    - **I**nstruct by providing clear and concise directions on how the agenda item will be executed.
    - **R**ecord the appropriate information gathered during the meeting, or ensure the information is recorded.
    - **S**tep the participants through the agenda item, using the appropriate information gathering process.
    - **T**rack time to ensure that the participants are using time appropriately.
    - **C**ontrol and resolve any dysfunctional behavior quickly and effectively.
    - **L**isten for off-topic discussions and redirect to a parking board to keep the meeting focused.
    - **A**ddress disagreements or conflicts that emerge.
    - **S**eek all opinions, and invite people to speak.
    - **S**ummarize the results.
19. Close the meeting.
    - Review the items covered in the meeting.
    - Confirm the decisions made.
    - Address outstanding issues.
    - Ensure that all actions have names and dates assigned.
20. Perform meeting follow-ups.
    - Ensure that meeting notes are documented and distributed.
    - Follow-up to hold people accountable to assigned actions.

What Do Masterful Meeting Participants Do?

The table that follows summarizes the Dos and Don'ts for participants in *Masterful Meetings*.

Do	Don't
Show up on-time, prepared to meet, having reviewed all materials provided in advance.	Show up late or unprepared.
Show respect to all present.	Speak while others have the floor, speak in a condescending tone, or verbally or physically attack another person.
Speak up when you disagree or don't understand.	Remain silent despite disagreement.
Speak positive points first.	Start with negative comments.
Share the air, giving others the opportunity to speak.	Dominate the discussion.
Share intent and all relevant information.	Hide intent, conceal information, or allow relevant issues to go unspoken.
Seek to understand by asking questions.	Disengage when you are not speaking.
Seek win-win solutions that satisfy all needs.	Insist your point of view is right and all others are wrong.
Stay focused on the topic and alert at all times.	Wander off topic or get engaged with other work (e.g., cell phone, PDA).
Stay present for the entire meeting.	Leave before the completion or scheduled completion of the meeting.
Exercise your meeting rights.	Have meeting rights violated without speaking up.

Special Topic: Meeting Types

To plan and hold *Masterful Meetings*, meeting leaders should recognize three basic meeting types: status meetings, working meetings, and strategy meetings. The meeting type is determined by whether the primary focus of the participants will be reviewing, creating, or direction-setting.

	"Status" Meeting	"Working" Meeting	"Strategy" Meeting
Meeting Focus	Review	Creation	Direction-setting
Meeting Flow	Primarily one-way	Primarily two-way	Primarily two-way
Typical Products	Information update, idea generation, feedback	Decision, issue resolution, action plan	Strategic direction, broad plan, priorities
Group Size	Unlimited	3–16	3–16
Typical Length	30–90 minutes	1–3 hours	1–3 days
Typical Frequency	Weekly	As needed	Quarterly

The Differences

- While status meetings are designed to review progress or gain feedback, working meetings are designed to create a decision, action plan, or some other product, and strategy meetings are designed to set a direction.
- Status meetings are primarily one-way communication and therefore can have three, thirty, or three hundred people.
- Working and strategy meetings, however, require two-way communication and should have a much smaller number of participants.
- And while status meetings tend to be relatively short since they are review meetings, working meetings and strategy meetings tend to be longer because creation typically takes more time.

A Common Problem with Status Meetings

Unfortunately, one of the most common problems with status meetings is that they become working meetings! That is, in the middle of the status meeting, the meeting leader discovers a problem and takes time during the status meeting to develop solutions.

Why is it a problem for a status meeting to include problem-solving? Let's create a mythical but fairly common example. Imagine a meeting with the meeting leader and ten others assembled for a status meeting.

Sample Status Meeting Problem

❑ Each of the ten members has been allotted five minutes to provide a status update as part of this one-hour meeting with ten minutes of cushion available as needed. What happens?

❑ By the fourth person, the ten-minute cushion has already been eaten up by two problem-solving detours.

❑ During each of the problem-solving detours, those not involved in the discussion put themselves on hold while waiting for the status meeting to continue.

❑ By the seventh person, there are only ten minutes left to split amongst the last four, so their reviews are rushed through.

❑ However, the tenth person has a pressing issue that, as it turns out, is more important than any of the others that took up the additional time!

You can prevent status meetings from becoming working meetings by using half the time to update statuses and identify issues and the other half to address the most critical issues identified.

Solving the Status Meeting Problem

❑ When an issue is identified in a status meeting that requires solving, the meeting leader should add this issue to the list of items to be addressed when the status meeting is over.

❑ Once the statuses of all items are complete, the leader should review the outstanding issues, allocate appropriate time among them, and continue to meet with those needed for the issue discussions.

❑ For all others, the status meeting is over!

A Common Problem with Working and Strategy Meetings

While working meetings are specifically designed to solve problems and strategy meetings to set direction, both meetings have the tendency to become *another* working meeting. Let's use an example of a working meeting convened to address problems with the hiring process.

Sample Working Meeting Problem

- The discussion starts with identifying several problems, including the cost and level of service from the organization's health insurance provider.

- One person suggests that we might have a different provider if there were more diversity within the HR and Benefits department and on the panel that does provider selection.

- A twenty-minute debate ensues concerning whether HR and Benefits and the panel need greater diversity.

While a case could be made that the team members are attempting to get at the root cause of the insurer selection, they may have lost sight of their core issue: problems with the hiring process and how to address them. They have instead detoured to a new topic: diversity in HR. As you will see in Part III, to prevent detours from the main topic, the meeting leader can respond as follows:

Solving the Working Meeting Problem

- "That may be a very valid point about diversity and something to investigate later. Can we put that on our list of potential issues to discuss, and get back to identifying other problems that directly affect our hiring process?"

An understanding of the differences between status meetings, working meetings, and strategy meetings will guide your selection of the appropriate purpose, products, and participants during preparation, which will be covered in Part II.

Summary: The Secrets to a Meeting Vision

In summary, the secrets to developing a vision of *Masterful Meetings* in your organization include the following:

Secret 1.   Define the problems to eliminate and their root causes.

Secret 2.   Establish your meeting vision that incorporates *Your Meeting Rights* and addresses the problems and root causes.

Secret 3.   Further define the vision by developing descriptions of the role of meeting leaders, the role of meeting participants, and the different meeting types.

Part II. Executing Masterful Meetings

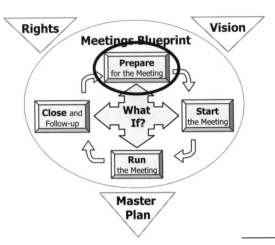

Chapter 3.
Preparing

Many meetings fail due to a lack of planning and preparation. This chapter provides you with a framework for planning and includes a comprehensive list of the items to cover in your preparation.

Checklist for Preparing

- ❑ *Decide the meeting purpose.
- ❑ *Define the meeting products.
- ❑ *Confirm the meeting is necessary.
- ❑ *Select the participants.
- ❑ *Identify probable issues.
- ❑ *Develop the agenda.
- ❑ Determine key processes and timings.
- ❑ *Determine meeting date, time, and location.
- ❑ *Develop and distribute the meeting notice.
- ❑ Hold preliminary discussions as needed in advance of the meeting.
- ❑ Prepare the room and other logistics.
- ❑ Prepare your opening words.

*Recommended for all meetings

Please note that not all items included in this chapter are needed for all meetings. For example, the preparation you would do for a one-on-one meeting with a subordinate is not the same as the preparation for a critical meeting with your supervisor and your supervisor's supervisor to gain approval for a controversial initiative.

For the checklist on the previous page, we have assumed that you are preparing for a critical meeting. Reduce the list as needed for the meetings you commonly lead. The asterisked items (*) indicate those actions that should be done in advance of every meeting, regardless of number of participants or importance.

Decide the Meeting Purpose

Start planning for your meeting by defining the four Ps of preparation: purpose, products, participants, and probable issues. Purpose defines the overall goal to be achieved. To identify your meeting purpose, consider the following questions:

- ❑ Why am I holding this meeting?
- ❑ At the meeting, what do I want to be achieved?

Sample Purpose Statements

- ❑ To define the actions we will take to improve a process.
- ❑ To develop a strategic plan for the organization.
- ❑ To ensure satisfactory progress is being made on the project.

Define the Meeting Products

The products are the specific items to be produced during the meeting that will define achievement of the purpose. Your desired products from the meeting may cover one or more of what I call the three Hs. You will want to identify what you want people to have in their:

- ❑ Hands (deliverables)
- ❑ Heads (knowledge)
- ❑ Hearts (beliefs)

To identify the products you want to result from the meeting, ask yourself one or more of the following questions:

- ❑ What specific tangible products or outcomes do I want to have produced when the meeting is over?

- ❏ Three months following the meeting, how will I know the meeting was successful?
- ❏ When the meeting ends, what do I want the participants to have in their hands, heads, and hearts?

<u>Sample Products</u>
- ❏ An action list with the steps to be taken, by whom, and when.
- ❏ A mission statement, guiding principles, broad goals, measurable targets, and specific strategies.
- ❏ Approval to move forward and high expectations of success.

Confirm the Meeting is Necessary

Meetings take time and tie up resources. Therefore, if a quality result can be achieved without holding a meeting, this is often preferred.

<u>Avoiding Status Meetings</u>
- ❏ If the meeting is truly "information only," consider distributing a memo instead or using voice mail.
- ❏ If little action has taken place between status meetings, consider making meetings less frequent.

<u>Avoiding Working Meetings and Strategy Meetings</u>
- ❏ Make analysis assignments and perform the analysis outside of a meeting.
- ❏ Document a preliminary decision in written form and circulate it for comment.

<u>Questions to Ask to Avoid Unnecessary Meetings</u>
- ❏ What is my purpose in calling the meeting?
- ❏ What products should result from the meeting?
- ❏ Is it possible to achieve the purpose and products without a meeting?
- ❏ Are the purpose and products worth the time and resources that the meeting will consume?

Select the Participants

Who are the right participants for the meeting? That depends on the meeting type.

<u>Participants for a Status Meeting</u>

- ❑ Those who need to know or their representatives.

<u>Participants for a Working or Strategy Meeting</u>

Each participant should:

- ❑ Understand the issue.
- ❑ Have a stake in the outcome.
- ❑ Be empowered to make a decision or recommendation.

As a group, the participants should:

- ❑ Represent diverse communication styles.
- ❑ Be knowledgeable of all relevant activities under study.
- ❑ Be cross-functional and representative of all groups with a major stake in the outcome.
- ❑ Be drawn from various levels within the organization structure (for example, managers, supervisors, and workers).

To help you identify the appropriate participants for a working or strategy meeting, consider the following questions:

- ❑ Who are the people who will be affected by the decision?
- ❑ What level of involvement should they have in the process?
- ❑ Whose perspectives, involvement, and buy-in are so critical that they should be at the table or represented by someone who is?

Identify Probable Issues

Once you know the purpose, products, and participants, the next step is to identify the probable issues that will likely affect the meeting's success. By identifying these issues in advance of the meeting, you can make adjustments to the process you will use to achieve the meeting's purpose.

Probable issues tend to have three different types.

Type	Definition	Example
General Issues	Questions and other items that will need to be covered by the agenda in order to create the products and achieve the meeting purpose.	What are other organizations doing with pay-for-performance?
Hot Concerns	Items that must be addressed but can derail the meeting if not handled well.	What do we do to prevent nepotism from entering into performance review decisions?
Red Herrings	Items that may come up that are not directly related to the topic and should not be addressed.	Are our benefits competitive?

To identify probable issues, ask yourself or poll one or more attendees for answers to the following questions:

How to Identify Probable Issues

❑ What are the topics that must be discussed to achieve the meeting purpose and create the products?

❑ What are the questions or concerns the participants will have about the purpose or products?

❑ What are potential red herrings we may encounter in achieving the purpose and products?

❑ What other potential problems may surface that may hinder us from achieving our purpose and products?

❑ How do we ensure that the meeting is not a waste of time?

Develop the Agenda

While purpose and products define the meeting's destination, the agenda defines the roadmap for getting there. The agenda identifies the steps you will take to achieve the purpose and products, taking into account the participants and probable issues.

In this section, I have included several sample agendas that you may find helpful in developing your own agendas.[1] Choose the agenda which most closely represents your defined purpose and desired products. These agendas are adapted with permission from *The Secrets of Facilitation*.

Sample Agendas

- ❑ Issue Resolution
- ❑ Process Improvement
- ❑ Project Planning
- ❑ Status Meetings
- ❑ Strategic Planning
- ❑ Team Development

Issue Resolution

Purpose

- ❑ Define an issue; identify alternative solutions; gain consensus on an alternative.

Products

- ❑ Selection Criteria.
- ❑ Alternative Definitions.
- ❑ Selected Alternative and Justification.

Agenda

A. Getting started.
B. What is the issue?
C. What criteria should we use in selecting a solution?
D. What are the alternatives?
E. What are the strengths and weaknesses of the alternatives?
F. Are there other alternatives that combine key strengths?
G. Which alternative should we select?
H. Review and close.

Process Improvement

Purpose
- ❑ Define the changes necessary to increase the efficiency and effectiveness of a business process.

Products
- ❑ New Process Description.
- ❑ Implementation Plan.

Agenda
- A. Getting started.
- B. How does the process work today?
- C. What are the overall goals of the process?
- D. What are the strengths of the current process?
- E. What are the problems and root causes?
- F. What are potential improvements?
- G. How might we prioritize these improvements?
- H. How will the new process work?
- I. How will we implement this new process?
- J. Review and close.

Project Planning

Purpose
- ❑ Identify the objectives of a project and the resources and timelines needed to complete it.

Product
- ❑ Project plan.

Agenda
- A. Getting started.
- B. Define the project purpose and objectives.
- C. Determine project scope and products.
- D. Identify critical success factors.
- E. Develop overall approach.
- F. Define resources, durations, dependencies, and schedule.
- G. Identify risks and contingencies.
- H. Review and close.

Status Meeting

Purpose
- ❑ Identify the status of a department, program, or project.

Products
- ❑ Updated status against plan.
- ❑ Actions to be completed.

Agenda
- A. Getting started. (one-minute check-in)
- B. Remind of overall department objectives.
- C. Review and update list of action items from prior meeting.
- D. Review status by team: accomplishments, priorities next period, and issues for later discussion.
- E. Prioritize discussion issues and allocate time.
- F. Resolve issues.
- G. Document action items for next meeting.
- H. Review and close.

Strategic Planning

Purpose
- ❑ Develop a shared vision and document the steps to achieve that vision.

Products
- ❑ Vision and mission statements.
- ❑ Goals, objectives, and guiding principles.
- ❑ Strategies and priorities.

Agenda
- A. Getting started.
- B. Review situation analysis.
- C. Develop goals, mission, and vision.
- D. Develop objectives.
- E. Identify critical success factors and barriers.
- F. Develop strategies and priorities.
- G. Document action plans.
- H. Review and close.

Team Development

Purpose
- ❑ Improve the ability of a team to work together.

Products
- ❑ Team vision and team norms.
- ❑ Our action plan.
- ❑ Our monitoring plan and accountability plan.

Agenda
- A. Getting started.
- B. What makes teams work?
- C. Our team vision.
- D. Our issues and barriers.
- E. Strategies to achieve our vision.
- F. Our monitoring plan.
- F. Our accountability plan.
- G. Review and close.

An Alternative Agenda Approach

The sample agendas indicate the purpose and products for the entire agenda. A different approach to agenda building is to indicate the purpose and desired outcome for each agenda item as shown in the sample that follows.

Agenda Item	Purpose	Desired Outcome
Capital budget.	Ensure that the capital budget is realistic and meets the needs of the organization.	Approval to proceed.
Financial update.	Report the current and projected financial condition.	Information only.
JV partner candidates.	Gain Board input on potential partners in joint venture.	List of potential partners.

This detailed, outcomes approach to agenda building is most helpful when there are numerous unrelated agenda items with each item resulting in an independent product.

Customizing an Agenda

You can customize the agenda to your particular situation based on your particular purpose, products, participants, and probable issues. Some examples follow:

Examples of How to Customize an Agenda

❑   If you are seeking to improve the performance review process, and you know there is a need for outside ideas, you might include a process step before "F. What are potential improvements?" such as "What are other organizations doing?"

❑   If you are putting together a project plan for implementing new customer-relationship-management software, you may be aware that the participants might be concerned about a lack of management support for the project (probable issue). Accordingly, you might include a step "H. How do we ensure management buy-in?"

❑   The agenda should be designed to create an "opening-then-narrowing" experience for the participants.

-   Early parts of the process should open the participants to the possibilities of what could be done. During this segment, many potential approaches should be identified.

-   Later parts of the process should narrow the possibilities of what could be done down to the strategies or recommendations that will be done.

Determine Key Processes and Timings

While the agenda defines what will happen in the meeting, the processes you use will determine how each agenda item will be accomplished and the amount of time required. In Chapter 6, you will find a detailed description of the following standard information gathering processes:

Sample Information Gathering Processes

- ❏ Listing
- ❏ Question & Answer
- ❏ Grouping
- ❏ Small Group Break-out
- ❏ Brainstorming
- ❏ Feedback
- ❏ Prioritizing

Estimating Timing

To estimate the duration for an agenda item, consider estimating the following:

- ❏ **Introduction**: How much time will it take to introduce the agenda item? Typically, this is one to five minutes, although some agenda introductions might take more time.
- ❏ **Unit Time:** How much time will it take to process one item? Typically this is one to ten minutes. For example, identifying each step in the performance review process might require only two minutes each.
- ❏ **Number of Units**: How many items will likely be identified? Let's assume for our example that we will have twenty steps in the performance review process.
- ❏ **Wrap-up**: How much time will it take to wrap up the discussion after all items have been identified? Let's assume that it will take another five minutes.

The mathematical formula for calculating the amount of time is as follows:

Time for an Agenda item
Introduction + (unit time x number of units) + wrap-up

For our example above, the amount of time required would be calculated as follows: Time = 5 + (2 x 20) + 5 = 50 minutes

Determine Meeting Date, Time, and Location

There are several factors to consider when deciding the date, time, and location of the meeting. The list below is a starting point, ordered by general relative importance. The items on the list and the order may vary for your situation.

Factors to Consider in Defining Date, Time, and Location

- ❑   When must the results of the meeting be known?
- ❑   Who are the people critical to the success of the meeting? And what are their available times and preferred locations?
- ❑   What rooms are available and when for the size of the group anticipated?
- ❑   What date, time, and location are convenient for you?

Date, Times, and Locations to Avoid

Avoid	Reason
Meeting on Monday morning or Friday afternoon.	People may be distracted from the weekend that is coming or the one that has just passed.
Meeting the day before a holiday or the day after a holiday.	People may be distracted by the holiday that is coming or the one that has just passed.
Starting a meeting right after lunch.	People tend to be more sluggish and have low energy and creativity.
Locations where participants can be distracted by activity outside the room.	Outside activity may reduce meeting productivity.
Rooms that are too small or too large for the audience.	Participants may be negatively affected by the environment.

Develop and Distribute the Meeting Notice

The meeting notice defines the key information that participants need in order to arrive prepared for the meeting. If possible, distribute the meeting notice at least a week prior to the meeting.

The Meetings Transformation Team
7/12/xx Gather 8:50 / End 11:30
1st Meeting—Conference Room A

Meeting Purpose

o   To confirm the project objective and gain agreement on how we will go about accomplishing our work.

Expected Products

o   Work process, operating norms, meeting schedule.

Proposed Agenda

8:50 Gather

9:00 Start

A.   Welcome, Purpose, and Agenda.

B.   Review the Team's Objective.

C.   Identify Critical Issues for Accomplishing the Team's Objective.

D.   Confirm the Team's Work Process (*The Master Plan*).

E.   Define Team Norms and Decision-making Method.

F.   Decide Logistics for Meetings.

G.   Begin Team Work Process (if time permits).

H.   Define Next Steps.

11:30 End

Invited Attendees

☐   Cleve C.—Team Leader   ☐ Ken M.

☐   Bill G.—Documenter   ☐ Vanessa R.—Executive Sponsor

☐   Trina J.   ☐ Andrea T.

In Advance: Review the team charter sent to you last week. Identify any specific meeting issues you would like to see addressed.

Bring to the Meeting: The team charter and list of issues.

Contents of the Meeting Notice

- ❑ Meeting purpose, expected products, and proposed agenda.
- ❑ Location, gathering time, and start and end times.
- ❑ Invited attendees.
- ❑ Recommended items to bring.

For recurring meetings such as status meetings, the meeting notice may not be necessary if the same items are covered in every meeting. For other meetings, the meeting notice may be verbal (e.g., voice mail) or in writing.

To help the meeting to start on time, make the first time on the agenda the gathering time followed by the actual start time. In this way, participants will know that they are expected to arrive early so that the meeting can start on time. If prior to the meeting there are items for participants to review or actions that need to be taken, distribute these in advance of the meeting as well.

Hold Preliminary Discussions as Needed

For critical or controversial meetings, it may be important to hold preliminary discussions with one or more participants in advance of the meeting. The list below provides a sample of reasons to hold preliminary discussions with one or more participants.

Hold Discussions Prior to the Meeting If . . .

- ❑ The issues are complex, and it would be helpful to have a small group create a starting-point solution.
- ❑ A critical mass is needed to move a decision forward, and you want to seek an initial agreement from a core group.
- ❑ One or more of the decision-makers have an inadequate understanding of the issue, and these misunderstandings could prevent a successful meeting.
- ❑ One or more participants stand to lose something if the meeting is successful, and it would help if they understood in advance what will likely happen in the meeting.
- ❑ One or more participants tend to point out problems, and it would be helpful to get them focusing on seeking solutions.
- ❑ One or more participants may attempt to change the agenda to surface their personal issues.

Prepare the Room and Other Logistics

Prior to the meeting, you will want to ensure that the room and other logistics are handled.

Items for Final Preparations
- ❏ Room setup (e.g., tables, chairs, food)
- ❏ Audio-visual (e.g., projector, teleconference)
- ❏ Room supplies (e.g., flipcharts, markers, post-its)

Prepare Your Opening Words

The final step in preparation is to prepare the words you will say to open the meeting. At the beginning of the meeting, you will want to thank, inform, excite, and empower. The next chapter provides details on these critical points.

Summary: The Secrets to Preparing

In summary, the secrets to preparing for *Masterful Meetings* include the following:

Secret 4. For your meeting, define the four Ps of preparation: purpose, products, participants, and probable issues. Validate that achieving the purpose and products requires and justifies holding a meeting.

Secret 5. Design an agenda to achieve the purpose and products, taking into account the participants and probable issues.

Secret 6. Use a variety of information gathering processes to make the meeting interesting and engaging.

Secret 7. Choose a meeting date, time, and location to maximize attendance and effectiveness.

Secret 8. Distribute a meeting notice in advance of the meeting to notify participants of the purpose of the meeting and to encourage participants to prepare for the meeting.

Secret 9. Be sure that the first time appearing on the meeting notice is the gathering time.

Secret 10. Hold preliminary discussions with people if the meeting is critical or includes controversial topics.

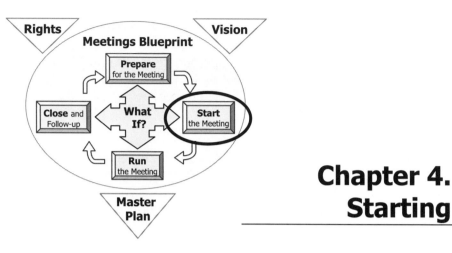

Chapter 4.
Starting

Meeting leaders often start meetings by reviewing the agenda—if they have one—and diving straight into the first agenda item. As a result, participants often aren't sure of the purpose of the meeting, the products to be produced, why the meeting is beneficial, or why the meeting should be important to them. In essence, meetings often begin with an ineffective start that can negatively affect the rest of the meeting.

This chapter covers the steps involved in starting a *Masterful Meeting*. The start of a meeting includes all the activities done before addressing the first work item on the agenda. Let's begin with the checklist for starting.

Checklist for Starting

❑ *Start the meeting on time.
❑ *Deliver the opening, including purpose and products.
❑ *Engage the participants.
❑ *Confirm the agenda.
❑ Review the ground rules.
❑ Review the parking boards.
❑ Make introductions if needed.

*Recommended for all meetings

The opening can take as little as five minutes and as long as forty-five minutes or more depending on the size of the group and the steps you use. You should adjust the list as appropriate for the meetings you lead. Those items asterisked (*) should be done to start every meeting, regardless of number of participants or importance.

Start the Meeting on Time

Getting the meeting started on time is a common challenge for meeting leaders. Unfortunately, most leaders "punish the punctual" by making those who arrive on time wait for those who are late. In some organizations, punishing the punctual is such a cultural norm that participants have learned to arrive late to avoid "being punished."

Of course it is difficult to start a meeting when key participants are tardy. Consider the following strategies to develop a culture and a habit of starting meetings on time.

Strategies for Starting on Time

❑ Get permission in advance from all participants to start the meeting at the appointed time.

❑ Make sure the meeting notice gives a gathering time and a start time. Most people pay attention to the first time they see.

❑ Consider setting the start time for meetings for five minutes after the hour or half-hour to allow time for people to leave one meeting and arrive at the next one.

❑ If someone else other than you will kick-off the meeting, make sure that person is aware of this role and that the two of you have agreed upon the time.

❑ Give a two-minute warning prior to the start to encourage people to take their seats.

❑ Consider gaining group agreement on a suitable penalty for arriving late such as a dollar donation to the party pool or responsibility for creating the meeting notes.

Deliver the Opening

The opening words set the tone, pace, and expectation for the rest of the meeting. Through the opening, you convey your vision of the meeting and the benefit to be gained. What should you say to make the opening effective?

Items to Cover in the Opening

❏ **Thank** the participants for coming.

❏ **Inform** them about the overall purpose of the meeting and the products that will result.

❏ **Excite** the participants by providing a vision of success and the benefits to them.

❏ **Empower** them by identifying the authority they have been given, the important role they play in the process, or the reason they were selected for the meeting.

How you deliver the opening is also important. When a leader speaks in a low monotone with little or no expression, participants can receive the message that the leader has limited interest in the meeting and low confidence that the meeting will achieve results. When the meeting leader speaks with excitement, interest, or passion about a topic, this feeling is conveyed to the participants. Consider delivering the opening in the following way:

Delivering the Opening Words

❏ Stand or sit tall; don't slouch.

❏ Make eye contact.

❏ Speak loudly, clearly, and with expression in your voice.

❏ Vary your tone.

❏ Use pauses for emphasis.

❏ Avoid speaking too fast or too slow.

❏ Be animated, using defined gestures.

❏ Avoid filler words (e.g., "ah," "er," and "um").

When you deliver the opening in this way, and the opening covers the items listed previously, it is more likely that the participants will understand why they are there, capture your vision and excitement about the meeting, and understand the role they play and the benefit to them. What follows is a sample opening.

<u>Sample Opening Words</u>

- ❏ I want to **thank** you all for agreeing to be a part of this meeting.
- ❏ Let me start by **informing** you about why we are here.
  - As you all know, we've been having significant difficulty with our performance review process.
  - There have been reports of wide differences among our departments on what is considered "meet" versus "exceeds" versus "far exceeds" expectations. A number of employees have commented that the review process is all about how well you are liked and not how well you perform. Additionally, we have had cases of people given high ratings just a few months before being fired because of poor performance. In summary, it doesn't appear that our performance review process is effective.
  - We have been called together to create a new process that will alleviate concerns like these.
- ❏ Why is this **exciting**?
  - If we are successful, and if we do our job well, it will, I hope, result in a process that our people can believe in, have faith in, and feel motivated by. And we all know that if our folks are motivated, it makes our jobs so much easier: fewer problems, fewer complaints, better morale, better performance, and a better bottom line means better bonuses for you, me, and everyone in the organization.
  - In addition, if we do our jobs well, we will have the thanks and gratitude of the senior staff and our peers for the significant improvements we will have made.
- ❏ I want to make sure you know that you have been **empowered** to get this job done.
  - Each of you was hand-picked by the Leadership Team to be part of this process.
  - They believe you have the knowledge as well as the vision for creating a much better process.
  - And they are looking forward to your recommendations.

Engage Participants (The Starting Question)

After delivering the opening, consider getting the participants immediately engaged. This engagement step involves everyone quickly and prepares them for the rest of the meeting.

How do you engage participants early in a meeting? For some teams, it is best to start with a question that is focused on the task at hand. For other teams, it may be more appropriate to start with a question that takes more of a people-focus. I recommend any one of the following:

Sample Initial Engagement Approaches
- ❑ Key Topics Approach
  - Think about the meeting purpose.
  - If we are going to accomplish this purpose, there are probably specific topics that you know we need to cover, specific issues that we have to address, or maybe specific ideas that we should discuss.
  - Let's build the list. If we are going to be successful today, what topics do we need to talk about?
- ❑ Personal Outcomes Approach
  - Let's assume this meeting was highly successful.
  - Think about the things that resulted, the outcomes that occurred, and the things that would make you say, "This was a great meeting."
  - Let's build the list. Given our purpose and products, what are the outcomes you personally would like to see come out of today's meeting?
- ❑ One-minute Check-in Approach
  - It has been several days since we were all together. Let's start with each person giving a quick one-minute check-in.
  - We were last together on [date]. Since that time, there probably have been one or more significant events that have occurred in your personal or professional life.
  - Consider the major events that have occurred and pick one that was significant for you. Let's go around the room. What is a significant event that has happened to you since we were last together?

The Starting Question
Each of the alternatives above is phrased to help participants visualize their answers by using a format known as the starting question.[2] To construct a starting question, use the three steps that follow:
- ❑ Start with an image building phrase (e.g., "Think about . . . Imagine . . . Consider . . . If . . .").

❑   Extend the image so the participants can see their answers. This usually takes two or three additional phrases.

❑   Ask the direct question that you desire to know.

When you ask questions in this way, participants typically visualize their answers and are immediately able to respond. If you simply ask the direct question, participants tend to become silent as they try to visualize answers. With the starting question, you make it easier for your participants to respond.

You should use starting questions at the beginning of a meeting to engage and also at any time you want participants to provide a lot of responses, such as when identifying steps in a process, brainstorming potential strategies, and listing alternatives.

The following table includes samples of direct questions and the much better starting question.

Direct Question	Sample Starting Question
How does the performance review process work today; what are the steps?	I would like to build a list of the steps in the current performance review process. Imagine that you have a great employee who, year after year, performs extremely well, and you want to make sure you cover all the bases in the performance review process to ensure that she receives a very positive review. Think about all the steps that you or she would have to take as part of the performance review process, all the things that would have to be done early in the year, late in the year, etc. Let's build the list. What are the steps in our current performance review process?
What are the problems with the current process?	Think about our last performance review cycle. Consider the things that were real problems, the things that frustrated you, the things that worked very poorly, or the things that were just real problems. What things made you say, "There's got to be a better way to do this!"? What are some of those frustrating problems with the current performance review process?
What are things	We are ready to build a list of things to do to

Direct Question	Sample Starting Question
we could do to improve the current process?	improve the performance review process. Look over the problems we need to fix. Consider things we could do to solve them. Think about things you have seen implemented in other places. Consider how technology might be used to improve the performance review process or ways that we can better organize to get the work done. Let your mind see all the possibilities that we might consider. Let's list some of the ideas that could be put in place to improve our process. Who wants to start?

Tips in Using the Initial Engagement Strategy

There are several tips that can help you be more effective with the initial engagement strategy.

- ❑ Name the person who will go first *before* you ask the question. As a result, this person will listen much more closely so as to be prepared to answer.

- ❑ Give the participants about a minute to jot down their responses *before* the first person responds. This way, people will have an opportunity to listen to the person speaking rather than be distracted by their own thoughts of what they will say.

- ❑ Use a "round-robin" by starting with the first person and going around the room. Round-robins avoid the awkward silence when people don't know who should go next.

- ❑ If you ask for personal outcomes or key topics, consider recording the responses on flip charts. You will be able to come back to the information after confirming the agenda.

Confirm the Agenda

After completing the opening statement and engaging the participants, the next step is to review the agenda and time limits if appropriate. The purpose of the review is to ensure that the participants understand how the meeting will flow and to gain confirmation that the agenda will address the purpose and products identified in the opening. To confirm the agenda, consider the following steps:

Steps to Confirm the Agenda[3]

- ❑ Review each step. Indicate the products that will be created, the timeframe, and how each step contributes to the overall meeting purpose.
- ❑ If you asked for personal outcomes or key topics as an initial engagement strategy, you can use the results to confirm the agenda.
  - After reviewing the agenda, review each personal outcome or key topic listed.
  - Ask the participants to identify under which agenda item each outcome or topic will likely be covered.
  - Circle any outcome or topic not covered by the proposed agenda.
  - After reviewing all outcomes or topics, go back to those circled items. Determine with the group whether these will be saved for a later meeting or if the agenda should be modified in order to ensure that they are discussed in the current meeting.
- ❑ Ask the participants to confirm the agenda.
  - To ask the question neutrally:
    - You might ask, "Given our purpose and products [as well as the outcomes or topics identified], do we need to make any modifications to the agenda, or can we proceed with the agenda as proposed?"
  - If you believe no modifications are needed to the proposed agenda:
    - You might ask the question this way, "Given our purpose and products [as well as the outcomes or topics identified], it appears our agenda meets our needs. Can we accept the agenda as proposed?"
    - You should raise your hand or nod your head as you ask the question to indicate the method to show agreement.
  - If you believe modifications are needed to the proposed agenda:
    - You might ask the question this way, "Given our purpose and products [as well as the outcomes or topics identified], I would like to propose just a few changes to the agenda. . . . Can we accept the agenda as amended?"
    - You should raise your hand or nod your head as you ask the question to indicate the method to show agreement.

- If other modifications are requested, you will be able to use your consensus-building strategies described in Chapter 9.

Review the Ground Rules

Ground rules provide a vehicle for gaining agreement on a set of behaviors that will guide how participants will interact with one another. Consider ground rules that guide what people do (procedural) and how they do it (behavioral). Some sample ground rules follow.

Sample Ground Rules

- ❑ Start and end on time.
- ❑ Everyone speaks.
- ❑ Have one conversation.
- ❑ No beeps, buzzes, or ringy-dingies.
- ❑ Meeting work only.
- ❑ Give benefits first.
- ❑ Take a stand.
- ❑ Be soft on people; hard on ideas.
- ❑ Share all relevant information.[4]
- ❑ Discuss un-discussable issues.[5]
- ❑ Explain reasoning and intent.[6]
- ❑ Use the parking boards.

While some teams may have worked together for some time and have established their own functional, unspoken ground rules, I have found that most groups benefits from a deliberate process of identifying in-bounds and out-of-bounds behavior. In using ground rules, consider the follow steps:

Steps in Using Ground Rules

- ❑ If you use the same room for most meetings, consider having ground rules permanently posted.
- ❑ If this is the first meeting of the team, review and explain each ground rule.
- ❑ If the team meets frequently, it may be adequate just to remind the team of the ground rules without reviewing each one.
- ❑ If the group has a frequent dysfunction (e.g., interrupting one another), consider adding a ground rule to address it (e.g., no interruptions).
- ❑ If the group will be meeting for one or more full days, consider asking the group to pick a recharge activity.

- The point of a recharge is to provide a simple tool for empowering participants to raise the energy level whenever needed.
- A recharge is a ten to fifteen second activity that combines something you say with something you do.
- Sample recharges include: the wave, Y-M-C-A, and the chicken dance.
- Once the participants select a recharge activity, anyone can call for it at anytime in the meeting when the energy is low.

Over time, ground rules can help team members become self-correcting. They will begin correcting themselves based on the ground rules that they have established and reinforced.

Review the Parking Boards

During a meeting, people will often bring up topics that are not directly related to the meeting's purpose or topics that will be covered in a later agenda item. Additionally, there will be times during the meeting that decisions will be made or follow-up actions identified. In each of these cases, consider "parking" the information on a flip chart or some other vehicle so that everyone is aware of the information.

For most meetings, I find three parking boards are particularly useful. At the beginning of the meeting, quickly review the purpose of the parking boards. (Note that the parking boards appear as the last ground rule, making for an easy transition to discussing them.)

Three Common Parking Boards

- ❑ Issues list—topics that need to be discussed later in the meeting or entirely outside the meeting.
- ❑ Decisions list—decisions made by the group that should be documented for future reference.
- ❑ Actions list—actions to be performed sometime after the completion of the meeting.

Make Introductions if Needed

If the meeting includes people who don't know one another, introductions may be appropriate. There are two types of introductions that I recommend, depending upon the situation. If most people generally know one another, but there are a few who don't, consider just the short form. The long form is more appropriate when the participants generally don't know one another.

<u>Short Form</u>
- ❏ Ask people to indicate their name, organization, and role.

<u>Long Form</u>
- ❏ Ask the participants to identify their name, organization, role, and a specific outcome or key topic most important to them.
- ❏ Consider recording the questions on a flip chart to ensure that people understand what they are being asked to say.
- ❏ Give participants time to write down their thoughts prior to the first person speaking.
- ❏ Set a time limit for each introduction (e.g., thirty seconds); consider using a clock with an alarm as a reminder of the time.

Summary: The Secrets to Starting

In summary, the secrets to starting *Masterful Meetings* effectively include the following:

Secret 11.   Achieve an on-time start by making the first time on the agenda the gathering time and gaining advance permission to start on time.

Secret 12.   Deliver a strong, effective opening by:
- Thanking the participants for coming.
- Informing them of the purpose and desired products.
- Exciting them about the benefits to them.
- Empower them by identifying the authority they have been given and role they play.

Secret 13.   Get the participants actively engaged early in the meeting by using a starting question focused on key topics, personal outcomes, one-minute check-in, or any other subject appropriate for the meeting.

Secret 14.   Gain buy-in to the agenda by linking the participants' personal outcomes or key topics to the agenda for the meeting.

Secret 15.   Use ground rules to identify in-bounds and out-of-bounds behavior.

Secret 16.   Establish parking boards to have a place to "park" decisions made, actions to be taken, or issues to be addressed at a later time.

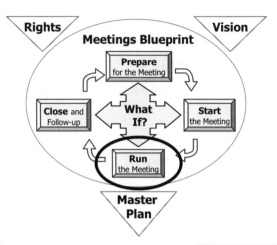

Chapter 5. Running the Meeting

Once you have gotten the meeting started, you will run the meeting by executing the agenda, and then close the meeting once all agenda items have been covered.

Checklist for Running a Meeting (FIRST CLASS)

For each agenda item:

- ☐ **F**ocus the participants by providing an explanation of how the item furthers the meeting's purpose.
- ☐ **I**nstruct by providing clear and concise directions on how the agenda item will be executed.
- ☐ **R**ecord the appropriate information during the meeting.
- ☐ **S**eek consensus before moving on.
- ☐ **T**rack time to ensure it is expended appropriately.

As needed:

- ☐ **C**ontrol and resolve any dysfunctional behavior quickly and effectively.
- ☐ **L**isten for off-topic discussions and redirect to a parking board to keep the meeting focused.
- ☐ **A**ddress disagreements or conflicts that emerge.
- ☐ **S**eek all opinions and invite people into the discussion.
- ☐ **S**ummarize and close the meeting.

This chapter covers the FIRST steps of the meeting leader.

Focus the Participants (Checkpoint)

At the beginning of every agenda item, take a checkpoint to get everyone on the same page.[7]

Taking a Checkpoint

- **Review**—Review quickly what has been done to date.
- **Preview**—Describe briefly what the group is about to do.
- **Big View**—Explain how the previewed agenda item fits into the overall meeting purpose.

The checkpoint serves to ensure that all participants are aware that a transition is taking place. It also helps participants understand why the agenda item is being done and how it fits into the purpose of the meeting. Finally, when you give a checkpoint at the beginning of every agenda item, the participants experience a smooth transition as you guide them through the meeting.

Sample Checkpoint

- We have just talked about how the performance review process works today. (*review*)
- Our next step is to identify the problems and root causes to those problems. (*preview*)
- This is important because if we identify the problems and root causes, we will be able to make sure that whatever solutions we create overcome these issues and result in a much better performance review process. (*big view*)

Instruct through Clear Directions (PeDeQs)

After the checkpoint, you may ask your meeting participants to engage in some type of activity such as brainstorming or working in small teams. Depending on the activity, the quality of the directions that you provide can affect the success for your participants. A key to running *Masterful Meetings* is delivering quality directions.

When giving directions, good meeting leaders describe what the participants are to do. However, *Masterful Meeting* leaders describe what to do, how to do it, and why doing it is important.

To ensure you cover the what, how, and why, consider giving directions by stepping through the PeDeQs.[8]

Providing Directions using PeDeQs

❑ Give the overall **P**urpose of the activity.

❑ When appropriate, use a simple **E**xample that is outside the topic area.

❑ Give general **D**irections, using verbal pictures and gestures.

❑ Give specific **E**xceptions and special cases.

❑ Ask for **Q**uestions.

❑ Ask a **S**tarting Question that gets participants visualizing the answers.

As an example, suppose you want the participants in the meeting to identify the problems that occur in the organization's performance review process. Along with identifying the problems, you also want to identify the symptom and root causes for each of the problems. The table to be completed follows, along with a sample PeDeQs dialogue.

Problem	Symptom	Root Cause

Sample Dialogue—PeDeQs

- ❏ We will use this table to help identify the problems, symptoms, and root causes related to the performance review process. *(purpose)*

- ❏ For example, if we wanted to drive our car, a problem might be a flat tire. The symptom might be that there is no air in the tire. The root cause might be that I haven't put air in the tire for a while. What else might be a root cause? *(example)*

- ❏ Well, we're not driving a car. We are analyzing the problems with the performance review process. Here's how we will do it. First we will list all the problems. Then, once we have identified the problems, we will then determine the symptom and root cause for each. (*directions*)

- ❏ Now, there are a few other things you need to know. While we are discussing problems, you may come up with a root cause. I will place it in the root cause list until we identify the problem related to it. Likewise, after we list all the problems and are talking about symptoms and root causes, you may mention a problem and I will add it to the bottom. (*exceptions*)

- ❏ Any questions? (*questions*)

- ❏ Okay, think about our last performance review cycle. Consider the things that were real problems, the things that frustrated you, and the things that worked very poorly, took too long, or were just real problems. What things made you say, "There's got to be a better way to do this!"? What are some of those frustrating problems with the current performance review process? (*starting question*)

Record Relevant Information

After providing the directions and getting the process initiated, record—or have someone record—the information provided by the participants. What should be recorded?

Items to Document in a Meeting

- ❏ **Decisions** made during the meeting.
- ❏ **Actions** assigned during the meeting.
- ❏ **Issues** that come up in the meeting to be discussed later.
- ❏ **Relevant analysis and comments** covered during the meeting.

Consider using a flip chart, LCD projection, or some other vehicle so that people can see the recorded comments. Why is it important for people to see what is recorded?

Benefits of Having Participants See What is Recorded

- ❏ Keeps everyone focused on the same topic.
- ❏ Discourages participants repeating comments previously made.
- ❏ Helps ensure that comments are recorded accurately.
- ❏ Allows participants to easily and accurately refer to comments previously made.

When recording information during the meeting, abide by the following recording rules to increase clarity and buy-in:

Recording Rules to Follow

Always write what was said before you respond.	⇒	Discourages you from recording only the points with which you agree.
Write what they said, not what you heard.	⇒	Empowers the participants by ensuring that you use their words; helps to prevent you from changing the words based on your opinion.
Write so they can read it.	⇒	If they can't read it, you lose the benefits described previously of having the participants see what is being recorded.

Seek Consensus Before Moving On

Once you believe you have completed an agenda item, it is important to gain consensus before moving on. Gaining consensus to move on prevents you, the meeting leader, from appearing to push a decision on participants before they are ready. How do you seek consensus?

Gaining Consensus to Move On

❏   Provide a brief summary of the information covered.

❏   Ask the participants, "Can we move on?"

The sample that follows provides a summary and then a check for consensus.

Sample Check for Consensus

❏   So we have identified twelve steps in the performance review process, including reviewing past accomplishments, rating performance areas, and identifying development needs. Are their other steps or can we move on? If you are ready to move on, give me a head nod.

Track Time against the Agenda

As the meeting progresses, you should track time against your plan to ensure that the meeting time is expended in the most appropriate way.

Steps for Tracking Your Time

❏   Be sure to have a timed agenda that shows the amount of time to spend on each item.

❏   Note the end time for each agenda item and determine the amount of time ahead or behind schedule.

❏   Make adjustments in the target time for each subsequent item as needed.

What should you do if the meeting falls behind? Strategies for addressing time issues are covered in Part III.

Summary: The Secrets to Meeting Execution

In summary, the secrets to running *Masterful Meetings* effectively include the following:

Secret 17. To get everyone on the same page and have a smooth flow to the agenda, take a checkpoint at the beginning of every agenda item.
- Review quickly what has been done to date.
- Describe briefly what the group is about to do.
- Explain how the previewed agenda item fits into the overall meeting purpose.

Secret 18. When giving directions, describe what to do, how to do it, and why doing it is important. Use the PeDeQs format.
- Give the overall **P**urpose of the activity.
- When appropriate, use a simple **E**xample that is outside the topic area.
- Give general **D**irections using verbal pictures and gestures.
- Give specific **E**xceptions and special cases.
- Ask for **Q**uestions.
- Ask a **S**tarting Question that gets participants visualizing the answers.

Secret 19. Record all key information provided during the meeting, including all issues, decisions, actions, and relevant analysis for future reference. Be sure to record the information without personal bias.

Secret 20. Before moving on the next agenda item, summarize the information covered and ask the participants, "Can we move on?"

Secret 21. Track time against your plan to ensure that the meeting time is expended in the most appropriate way.

Seven Common Information Gathering Processes

	Purpose	Sample Use
Listing	Create a list of details or known information.	What are the problems that occur in meetings?
Grouping	Categorize information.	Given these twelve different problems, what are the three to five major categories they represent?
Brainstorming	Generate ideas.	What could we do to improve our meetings?
Prioritizing	Identify items of greatest importance.	With twenty possibilities, which ones should be given priority?
Question & Answer	Identify and respond to specific concerns.	What questions or issues do we have about this?
Small Group Break-out	Increase participation, efficiency, group energy and focus.	Can we break into small groups and have each group develop answers for one of the issues?
Feedback	Collect opinions and input.	Let's take a minute to identify the strengths and concerns about this suggestion.

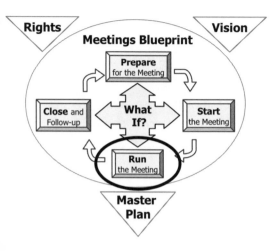

Chapter 6.
Gathering
Information

While running each agenda item in a meeting, you routinely use some method to get information out on the table. These methods for getting information are generally called information gathering processes.[9]

Examples of Information Gathering Processes

❑ In a meeting to generate ideas, a brainstorming process may be used in which participants provide as many ideas as possible before going back and analyzing each one.

❑ In a problem solving meeting, a listing process to identify the problems may be followed by small-group breakout to develop solutions.

Nearly every agenda item in a meeting uses some type of information gathering process, for if there were no need to gather any information, the meeting might as well be accomplished through voice mail or an e-mail sent to every participant.

Unfortunately, most meeting leaders do not plan the processes that they will use for each of their agenda items. As a result, during meetings, the most frequent processes used are "listing" and "presentation-then-questions." When you use the right process to address the specific need and when you vary the way the processes are done, meetings are more focused, more productive, and much more interesting for the participants.

The table on the opposite page summarizes seven common processes described in this chapter.

Listing to Gather Details

Purpose: Create a list of details or known information.

Sample Use: What are common problems that occur in meetings?

1. Title your flip charts (or other recording device) ahead of time.

2. Describe the activity and purpose.
    - "Our next step is to identify common problems that occur in meetings. This step is important because by identifying the frequent problems that occur in our meetings, we will be able to develop a plan for addressing our specific problems."

3. Give the general directions with an example if necessary.
    - "I would like for us to go around the room, starting with Pat, and have all of us identify one problem we have had in meetings. After we have gone around once, we'll come back and ask if anyone has other problems that haven't already been said. If it is your turn and you can't think of a different problem, just indicate one that has been said that you find most common. For example, you might say, 'ditto to number one or ditto to number seven.' Any questions?"

4. Ask a starting question to help the group visualize their answers.
    - "Think about a meeting that you attended in the last sixty days that was a really bad meeting. Think about the things that didn't go well, the difficulties in the meeting, the problems that occurred, the things that happened that made the meeting not nearly as effective as it could have been. Let's build a list of those problems. Pat, get me started. What are problems that occur in meetings?"

5. Record the responses you receive from the participants.

The diagram on the next page provides a sample of a flip chart that might result from the listing exercise described.

Problems with Meetings

1. No agenda.
2. Minimal participation.
3. Going off track.
4. Side conversations.
5. No decisions.
6. No results.
7. Sarcastic comments.
8. Too many agenda items.
9. No real purpose to meet.
10. One person dominating.
11. Too much detail.
12. No follow-up.

Grouping to Categorize (Affinity Diagram)

Purpose: Categorize information

Sample Use: Given these twelve problems, what are the three to six
               major categories that they represent?

1. To prepare for grouping, title your flip charts (or other recording device) ahead of time. Arrange the information to be categorized near the front of the room for easy viewing and marking.

2. Describe the activity and purpose.
   - "Our next step is to take the items that we have created and group them into categories. We might end up with anywhere from three to six categories. By doing this, we will be better able to develop solutions for the category instead of solutions for the individual problems."

3. Give the general directions.
   - "I will step through the items one by one and ask the group to name the category that the item should go in. If the category doesn't already exist, we will create a new one. At the end, we will review the categories to make sure we are all comfortable."

4. Read the first item and ask the participants to define the category for it. You might suggest a category for the first item to get the participants started.
   - "The first item says: 'No agenda.' Let's name the category in which 'No agenda' would be included. What would the category name be?"
   - "It sounds like this first one has to do with preparation; does that sound like a reasonable category?"

5. Write the category name on a flip chart and label it "A." Place an "A" next to the first item in the brainstorm list to indicate which group it was put in. Use a pen color different from the color used to create the original list so that the category label stands out.

6. Go to the next item on the original list. Ask the participants to determine whether it belongs in an existing group or whether a separate group is needed.
   - "The second item is 'Minimal participation.' Should we group this with preparation or should it go in a different category?"

7. If the item belongs in an existing group, label the item with the category letter. If the item belongs in a new group, ask the participants for the name of the category, give the category a letter, and write the letter next to the item.

8. Continue steps 6 and 7 until all items on the original list have been categorized.

9. Review the groups to determine if additional consolidation or category splitting is appropriate.
   - "Let's review what we have done to make sure the groups make sense. At this point, we have three items in each of our four categories. Do these seem appropriate?"

The following chart is a sample of output from the grouping exercise described above:

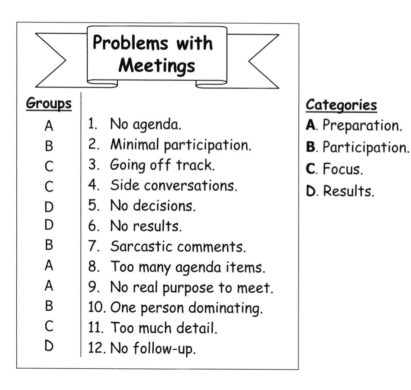

Problems with Meetings

Groups		Categories
A	1. No agenda.	**A**. Preparation.
B	2. Minimal participation.	**B**. Participation.
C	3. Going off track.	**C**. Focus.
C	4. Side conversations.	**D**. Results.
D	5. No decisions.	
D	6. No results.	
B	7. Sarcastic comments.	
A	8. Too many agenda items.	
A	9. No real purpose to meet.	
B	10. One person dominating.	
C	11. Too much detail.	
D	12. No follow-up.	

Brainstorming to Generate Ideas

Purpose: Generate ideas.

Sample Use: What could we do to improve our meetings?

1. Title your flip charts (or other recording device) ahead of time.

2. Describe the activity and purpose; be sure to encourage creativity and out-of-the-ordinary ideas.
   - "Our next step is to brainstorm potential improvements to our meetings. This is important because we don't want to continue to have bad meetings. Instead, we want to come up with solutions that can help us ensure that our meetings are effective, efficient, and achieve results."

3. Set a time limit and describe the general directions with an example if necessary; offer a response format if appropriate.
   - "We are going to take five minutes to do a round of intense brainstorming. I would like for us to go around the room, starting with Joe, and have each person give me one thing we could do that would move us toward our vision of *Masterful Meetings*. If you can, give me a 'verb-object' such as 'Implement this. Develop that.'"
   - "We will probably go around three or more times, so if you can't think of anything the first time, just say 'pass.'"

4. Prohibit judgment of any type on an idea. If the idea does not meet the objective, record it anyway. Remind the participants of the objective and keep moving.
   - "Since we want to keep the creative juices flowing, it is important that during this phase we don't spend any time judging or analyzing the ideas. I will be writing as fast as I can, and we will be moving quickly from person to person. If you find yourself at any point thinking, 'That won't work,' ask yourself, 'What will work? How can I improve on it?' Some of the best ideas start out as impractical suggestions."

5. Ask a starting question to help the group visualize their answers.
   - "Let's go back to our list of problems and the categories. These are the things we have to fix. Think about things you've seen other companies do, things that you have thought about us do-

ing, and things we could do to make our meetings much better. Joe, get me started. Let's build a list of some of the things we could do to improve our meetings? What are some of those things?"

6. Record responses.

7. Keep a steady pace. At this point, go for quantity rather than quality of ideas. The more ideas the better. Use a lot of fill-in words if necessary.
   - "Give me more. Who's next? More ideas, more ideas. . . . What other ways could we improve our meetings?"

8. End the brainstorming segment when the time limit is reached or when there is a round in which everyone passes. Ask for any last thoughts before closing.
   - "We have reached our time limit. Any last minute ideas to add?"

9. Always follow a brainstorming session with some type of grouping or prioritization activity to highlight the jewels.

The sample flip chart that follows represents information that could have been generated as a result of the brainstorming session described above:

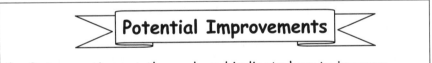

Potential Improvements

1. Rate meetings at the end, and indicate how to improve.
2. Provide managers training on running better meetings.
3. Provide a resource guide on how to be a better meeting participant.
4. Have quarterly awards for best run meeting or best meeting leader or most productive results.
5. Have an annual meeting feedback survey where meeting leaders get rated on the meetings they run.
6. Grant people meeting rights.
7. Track progress on how we are improving meetings.

Prioritizing: The Dot Method (Multi-Voting)

Purpose: Identify items of greatest importance.

Sample Use: With twenty possibilities, which ones should be given priority?

There are a number of methods to prioritizing, including raising hands, secret ballots, using dots, and weighted scoring. I describe the dot method below.

1. Prepare your flip charts (or other recording device) ahead of time.
2. Describe the activity and purpose.
   - "Our next step is to prioritize these improvements in order to identify the ones that we should begin implementing first."
3. Give general directions.
   - "We will start by identifying the most important criteria to use in our prioritization. I will then give everyone a set of colored dots. You should place your dots on those improvements that you feel will have the greatest effect on our meetings. The improvements with the most dots will be the ones that we will consider for initial implementation."
   - "Before we start voting, however, we will have a special lobbying period. See, if I were participating in the voting, I would want everyone to vote the way I would vote. I would hate it if, after applying dots, the improvement I believed was the most important received only my vote. The lobbying period is intended to address this. Before anyone votes, each of us will have one minute to share with the whole group what we believe are the most important items to get votes. After everyone who wants to has taken their sixty seconds to lobby, we will then vote."
   - "So to recap: first, we will talk about the criteria to use in selecting our priorities; second, we will have a lobbying period; and finally, we will vote and review the outcome. Any questions?"

4. Suggest criteria to the team and ask for other criteria before seeking acceptance.
   - "There are three criteria that we typically like to keep in mind when prioritizing. The level of impact is perhaps most important: what will be the impact of this improvement on the quality of our meetings? High, medium, or low? Probability of success is our second criterion. If we choose to implement this improvement, how likely is it that we will succeed given the nature of the improvement, our skill sets, and other factors? Finally, we look at cost-effectiveness. How cost-effective is this improvement compared to others in terms of providing the greatest bang for the buck? Are there other criteria you suggest we keep in mind?"

5. After establishing the criteria, provide an opportunity for each person to lobby the group for support.
   - "We have talked about the criteria. Now, before we use our dots, we will all have the option of taking one minute to indicate those improvements we think should be given highest priority and explain why. The 'why' is the most important part because it will give each of us a better understanding of the value of the improvement. I would like to start with Jamie and go around the room. Each person can 'pass or play.' Jamie, what do you think? Would you like to pass or lobby the group?"

6. Distribute and explain the dots. Distribute a number of dots equal to twenty to thirty percent of the total number of items. To get a wider range of priority scores, consider using multicolored dots.
   - "Now that lobbying is complete, let's determine our priorities. You have been given five dots. Three dots are red; the rest are blue. Place the red dots on the three improvements that you believe are the most important. Place the blue dots on two other improvements that you would like to see happen as well. The red dots count for three points each, while the blue dots each count for one point."
   - "You will have five minutes to place your dots on the ones that you feel are the best. You *cannot* place more than one dot on an item. As you are voting, keep in mind the criteria we decided on. Any questions?"

7. Review the results and ask for consensus to move forward with the voted priorities. If you do not have consensus, use consensus-building strategies described in Part III to resolve the issue.
   - "Of the fifteen improvements resulting from the brainstorming activity, it appears that only seven received any votes at all. Of the seven, the top five vote-getters are clearly the winners."
   - "While we may be able to implement all of these, it is clear that the ones to start with are the following. . . . Let's go around the room and check for consensus. Give me a head nod if you're okay with these priorities."

The sample flip chart that follows represents information that could have been generated as a result of the prioritization session described above:

Priorities

3333331
(19)

1. Rate meetings at the end, and indicate how to improve.

3333311
(17)

2. Provide managers training on running better meetings.

33331
(13)

3. Provide a resource guide on how to be a better meeting participant.

31111
(7)

4. Have quarterly awards for best run meeting or best meeting leader or most productive results.

1
(1)

5. Have an annual meeting feedback survey where meeting leaders get rated by their people.

33111
(9)

6. Grant people meeting rights.

1
(1)

7. Track progress on how we are improving meetings.

("3" represents red dots, which count for three points each; "1" represents blue dots, which count for one point each. The total score is shown in boldface in parentheses.)

Question & Answer

Purpose: Identify and respond to specific concerns.
Sample Use: What questions or issues do we have about this?

To maximize the question and answer period, consider gathering all questions at one time, grouping the questions, and then having the answerer respond to a group of questions all at once. This approach helps to ensure that the most critical questions get answered first, and it provides a full view of all questions so that the time spent responding can be better managed.

1. Title your flip charts (or other recording device) ahead of time.

2. Describe the activity and purpose.
    - "Now that we have heard an expert speak on transforming meetings inside our organization, let's take a minute to identify the additional questions we want answered. This will allow us to identify all the questions at once and will give our speaker a chance to cover all the questions."

3. Divide into teams and select a leader.
    - "To do this, let's quickly divide into teams where we are seated. Andrea, Bill, and Vanessa, you will make up team one. Team two will include . . ."
    - "We need team leaders, so I would like for the person from your team sitting closest to me right now to serve as the team leader. Team leaders, please grab the writing pad and the marker that is at your table."

4. Give directions to the teams, including a two-minute time limit to record their most important questions on the writing pad.
    - "Team leaders, you will have two minutes in total to identify the most important questions that your team would like to see answered as a result of this presentation. Please use the marker and pad you were given and have only one question per sheet. When the two minutes are up, your pen should be capped and in the air. I will count down the time for you. Any questions?"

5. Ask a starting question to help the group visualize their answers.
    - "We just heard a presentation on strategies used by other organizations to improve meetings. Think about the things you

heard, the things you want to hear more about, and the specific questions that will help us design our own meetings transformation process. Take the time in your teams to write down those questions. Remember, one question per sheet. What are the key questions you would like to see answered? You have two minutes, starting now."

6. Use the grouping technique to create question categories by reviewing and grouping each sheet.

   - "It looks like we have six pages from the first group. The first one says, 'Has any organization you know of actually granted their employees meeting rights?' Let's create a category for this question, and let's give the category a name so that other questions similar to it will go in this same category. What would be an appropriate name for the first category? Okay, so we have Category A—Empowering. What about the second question? It says . . . Does this go with the empowering category or does it need a new category? Okay, let's go to the next question . . ."

7. Do a checkpoint and turn it over to the speaker to respond to the questions.

   - "We have identified the key questions we want to have answered and grouped them into five categories. Now let's turn it over to the speaker who will use our last thirty minutes to cover each group of questions. This will help to ensure that we get to the most important questions. And if time remains, we will open it up to the floor for additional questions. So, let's hear from our speaker who will tell us which group of questions to tackle first . . ."

Small Group Break-out

Purpose: Increase participation, efficiency, group energy, and focus.

Sample Use: Can we break into small groups and have each group develop answers for one of the problem categories?

Break-out groups are especially appropriate when the agenda calls for a facilitated process to be performed several times (for example, to identify solutions to the four categories of meeting problems).

1. Let the participants know that they are about to break-out.
   - "In a minute we will be breaking-out into groups to identify up to three priority strategies for addressing each of our categories of problems with meetings."

2. Complete the first element with the entire group.
   - "Before we break-out into groups, however, I would like for us to tackle one of the categories together so that everyone is aware of what we are trying to do, how to do it, and what the product looks like that each team will create."
   - "Let's work together on . . . We will first spend five minutes brainstorming solutions. We will then have a lobbying period to discuss the solutions each of us believes have the greatest potential. Then we will vote to select our top three. Let's start by . . ."

3. Divide into teams.
   - "We have three additional categories of problems, so let's break into three teams by counting off by threes. . . . If you would now, let's have all the 1s over here, all the 2s over there . . ."

4. Appoint team leaders, scribes, and reporters.
   - "We need to appoint team leaders. I would like the person on your team whose birthday is closest to today to be the team leader. So let's quickly go around and give birthdates—no years, please: we have to protect the guilty. Now that we have team leaders, I would like the person to the team leader's right to serve as the scribe and the reporter for the break-out."

5. Give final directions to the teams covering the timeframe, product, process for creating it, and a progress milestone (e.g., how far you should be when half the time has passed).
   - "Before you start, let me review the instructions. You will have thirty minutes to identify up to three top strategies for addressing the category of meeting problems assigned to your team. The process is to first spend five minutes brainstorming solutions. You will then have a lobbying period to discuss the solutions that each team member believes have the greatest potential. Then you will vote to select up to three. As a milestone for you, by the end of twenty minutes, you should be wrapping up the lobbying period. Any questions?"

6. Monitor the activity.
   - As the break-out teams are working, you will want to rotate from team to team to monitor the activity. Specifically, you will want to ensure that each team is progressing as expected, that the deliverable items are reasonably close to what is desired, and that the timeframe is being met.

7. Have each team report their results.
   - "Now that we are done, let's hear from each team. You will have three minutes to describe the solutions that your team developed and to explain why these are the most appropriate."

Feedback (Pro-con Chart)

Purpose: Collect opinions and input.

Sample Use: Let's take a minute to identify the strengths and concerns about this suggestion.

Feedback is an important part of learning and improvement. Unfortunately, when the meeting leader gives a suggestion, it is not unusual for everyone to say, "Yes, good idea," or when someone else gives an idea, it is not uncommon to hear, "No way, that won't work." While in the first case there might appear to be full agreement when there is not, in the second case, one person's initial negative comment can completely derail a potentially beneficial idea. Consider the following when seeking feedback on an idea or when evaluating an activity:

1. Title your flip charts (or other recording device) ahead of time.

2. Describe the activity and purpose.
   - "Ken has just shared his view on how we might address a manager who chronically has bad meetings. Let's get some input on this."

3. Provide the general directions.
   - "Let's affirm Ken's contribution by quickly going around and saying what you like about the idea. Then we'll talk about concerns and ways to improve."

4. Start with strengths. Ask a starting question. Check-mark similar comments.
   - "So, let's start with strengths. I would like to go around the room, starting with Trina. I would like each one of you to identify one thing you liked about the suggestion. If someone has already said the thing you like, feel free to say 'Ditto number one,' and I'll put a check mark there to indicate another person agreed with the comment. So think about the suggestion Ken made, how it might work, and the benefits we could achieve by doing it. Let's build the list. Trina, get me started. What do you like about what Ken said?" (Note: In some cases, it will be appropriate to have just two or three comments on strengths instead of comments from the entire group. This is especially true if there is a large number of participants or if the suggestion is minor.)

5. Move on to concerns or ways to improve. Have participants randomly indicate suggestions.
   - "We've talked about strengths. Let's move on to concerns or ways to improve. I would like to open it up. We do not have to go in any order. As you heard Ken give the suggestion, you might have had concerns about it or thoughts on how to improve on it. Let's jump in. Who wants to go first?"

6. If appropriate, go back and review each improvement suggestion and ask for a show of hands for the number of people who support each. If it is a small group, you might count the individual hands. If it is a larger group, it might be faster to estimate the percentage of people who agree.
   - "Let's now go back over each improvement suggestion. I would like to get a rough indication of the level of support for each one. As I read each suggestion, please raise your hand if you agree with that suggestion. The first says . . . How many people agree that this suggestion would have improved the meeting? That looks like about eighty percent. Let's move onto the next. . . ."

7. In some cases, having information on the number of people who support each improvement will be adequate. If full consensus is needed, you will use the consensus-building strategies described in Chapter 9.

Summary: The Secret to Gathering Information

In summary, the secret to gathering information effectively in *Masterful Meetings* includes the following:

Secret 22. For each agenda item, use the appropriate process based on the purpose of the agenda item.

Listing .... Create a list of details.

Grouping .... Categorize information.

Brainstorming.......... Generate ideas.

Prioritizing .... Identify items of most importance.

Q&A .... Identify and respond to specific concerns.

Break-out............... Increase participation, efficiency, group energy, and focus.

Feedback .... Collect opinions and input.

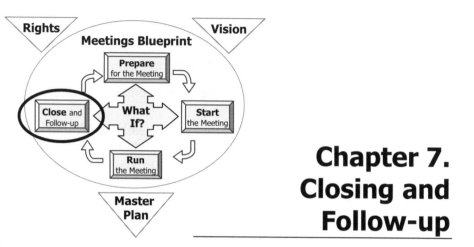

Chapter 7.
Closing and
Follow-up

Once all agenda items have been covered, it is time to close the meeting. Prior to closing, there are a number of items to be covered, and after closing, follow-up is often needed. This chapter covers both closing and following-up.

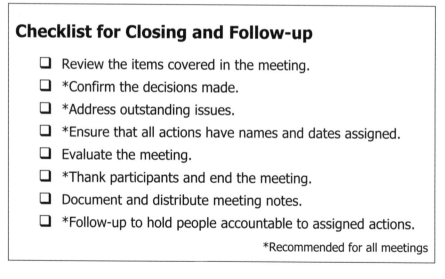

Checklist for Closing and Follow-up

☐ Review the items covered in the meeting.
☐ *Confirm the decisions made.
☐ *Address outstanding issues.
☐ *Ensure that all actions have names and dates assigned.
☐ Evaluate the meeting.
☐ *Thank participants and end the meeting.
☐ Document and distribute meeting notes.
☐ *Follow-up to hold people accountable to assigned actions.

*Recommended for all meetings

As with prior chapters on preparing and starting, not all meetings will require all the closing and follow-up steps. The closing can take as little as five minutes and as long as forty-five minutes or even longer depending on the size of the group and the steps you use. You should adjust the list as appropriate for the meetings you lead. Those items asterisked (*) should be done for every meeting regardless of the number of participants.

Review Items Covered in the Meeting

Prior to ending the meeting, go back to the agenda and summarize all of the activities completed during the meeting.

- ❑ The review provides the participants with a reminder of what was done. It also can provide a sense of accomplishment.
  - "Let's step through the agenda and identify what has been accomplished during this meeting."
- ❑ If key topics or participant outcomes were identified, review each one to ensure coverage.
  - "Let's also ensure that each key topic was covered or if we need to add any of these to the agenda for our next meeting."

Confirm Decisions Made

Next, review the Decision List, the parking board used to record decisions.

- ❑ The goal of the decision review is to remind the team of the decisions that have been made.
  - "Let's next review the decisions we made during this meeting. I will walk through each one. Stop me if any one of them is not recorded correctly."
- ❑ Following the meeting, participants may be asked why specific decisions were made. To prepare participants for the discussion, consider taking time in the closing to document the benefits of each decision.
  - "To help ensure that we all understand why each decision was made, let's take a moment to add one or two bullet points to each decision to document the benefit we expect to gain. Let's start with this first one, which says . . . Think about the benefits to be gained from this. Let's list one or two of these."

Address Outstanding Issues

The open issues list was the place that you parked topics that arose during the meeting that either needed to be covered at a later time or were completely irrelevant to the meeting. At the end of the meeting, it is important to clear all remaining items off of the open issues list.

<u>Questions to Ask to Clear the Issues List</u>
As a systematic way to quickly process the issue list, ask these questions in the following order for each issue:

❑ "Have we covered it?" (If so, move on to the next issue.)

❑ "Do we need to cover it?" (If not, move on to the next issue.)

❑ "Do we need to cover it now?"
- Yes: Set a time limit and lead the discussion.
- No: Move the issue to the action list.

Assign Actions

The actions list contains activities to be performed sometime after the completion of the meeting.

Action	Who	When
1.		
2.		
3.		

<u>Questions to Ask about Actions</u>

❑ "Does this action still need to be accomplished?" (If not, discard it and move on to the next action.)

❑ "Who should do it?"
- It is not appropriate to assign an action to someone not in the room.
- If the action is best performed by someone outside the room, assign it to a person of authority in the room who will then ask the other person to perform the action.

❑ "By what date will you have it completed?"
- If appropriate, let the person responsible for the action set the date for completion.

Evaluate the Meeting

Feedback from meeting participants can provide valuable insights on how to continuously improve meetings. Consider combining the feedback steps described in Chapter 7 with a brief rating system.

1. Start with strengths.

   ❏ "Let's start with strengths. I would like to go around the room, starting with Andrea. I would like all of us to identify one thing we liked about the meeting and the way we worked. If someone has already said the thing you like, feel free to say 'Ditto number one.'"

   ❏ "So, think about the things you liked about the meeting, the things that went well, the times that people seemed to be engaged, and the things that really worked. Let's build the list. Andrea, get me started. What did you like about the meeting? What went well?"

2. Rate the meeting.

   ❏ "Let's rate the meeting on our key criteria. Remember our rating system: 3 means the meeting was well done, 2 means it was adequate, and 1 means it was insufficient. How would you rate . . ."

Preparation and Start?	The meeting notice, participants preparation, on-time start, clear purpose, and appropriate agenda.
Staying Focused?	Keeping on track and at the appropriate level of detail.
Group Dynamics?	Working together, everyone engaged, handling conflict, and minimizing dysfunction.
The Results?	Good decisions, clear actions, and follow-up plan.
Overall Rating?	

3. Move on to ways to improve.

   ❏ "We've talked about strengths and rated the meeting. Let's move on to ways to improve. I would like to open it up. We do not have to go in any order. Take a look at the ratings, especially the lower ones. Think about the things that could have happened that would have improved these ratings: things we should consider doing differently next time. What would you suggest that we do differently that would have made the meeting even better? Who wants to go first?"

4. Review each improvement suggestion and ask for a show of hands of those who support each.

    ❑ "Let's go back now over each improvement suggestion. I would like to get a rough indication of the level of support for each one. As I read each suggestion, please raise your hand if you agree with that suggestion. The first says . . . How many people agree that this suggestion would have improved the meeting? That looks like about eighty percent. Let's move on to the next . . ."

Thank Participants and End the Meeting

Finally, end the meeting by expressing to the participants your appreciation for their attendance, reminding them of the next steps, and adjourning the meeting.

❑ "Thank you for participating in this meeting."

❑ "You should be receiving documentation of this meeting within seven days."

❑ "Our next meeting is on [date] at [time] in this same room. I will see you all then."

❑ "This meeting is officially adjourned!"

Document and Distribute Meeting Notes

What should be documented and included in the meeting notes? Consider the following:

Items to Document in Meeting Notes

❑ *Decisions made during the meeting.

❑ *Actions assigned during the meeting.

❑ Issues that come up in the meeting to be discussed later.

❑ Relevant analysis and comments covered during the meeting.

While not all items are required in the documentation that follows every meeting, the asterisked (*) items should always be documented.

The final documentation will also include notes added by the documenter to add clarity or build context for the reader. Consider italicizing notes added by the documenter to differentiate these notes from information provided by the participants. An example of meeting notes appears on the next page.

Follow-up to Hold People Accountable

To ensure that actions assigned during the meeting are accomplished, consider follow-up actions such as the following:

Strategies to Encourage Follow-up on Actions

❏   In the body of the letter or e-mail that accompanies the meeting notes, remind the participants that actions are included that need to be completed prior to the next meeting.

❏   Several days before the next meeting, distribute a letter or e-mail that highlights the actions to be completed prior to the next meeting.

❏   On the agenda for the next meeting, include a review of prior actions as the first or second agenda item.

❏   At the next meeting, ask people to report on those actions due to be completed.

- Give praise and applause to those items completed on time.
- For those items not completed, get a revised date from the person by when the item will be completed.

If follow-up appears to be a problem, consider having the team agree on a consequence list (e.g., twenty push-ups, buying everyone lunch, providing the minutes for the next three meetings) when an assigned date for an action is missed more than once.

Sample Meeting Notes

The Meetings Transformation Team
Meeting Notes from 7/12/xx

The Meetings Transformation Team held its first meeting on xx/xx/xx from 9:00 a.m. to 11:30 a.m. The meeting was held in Conference Room A. Attendees of the meeting were the following people:

- Cleve C.—Team Leader
- Bill G.—Documenter
- Trina J.
- Ken M.
- Vanessa R.—Executive Sponsor
- Andrea T.

The following are the meeting notes from the meeting. *Items appearing in italics indicate information added by the documenter for clarity or to provide context.*

A. Welcome, Purpose, and Agenda

Following the welcome, the Team Leader presented and gained agreement on the following purpose and agenda for the meeting.

Meeting Purpose

To confirm the project objective and gain agreement on the work process and our operating norms.

Meeting Agenda

A. Welcome, Purpose, and Agenda.

B. Review the Team's Objective.

C. Identify Critical Issues for Accomplishing the Team's Objective.

D. Confirm the Team's Work Process (*The Master Plan*).

E. Define Team Norms and Decision-making Method.

F. Decide Logistics for Meetings.

G. Begin Team Work Process (if time permits).

H. Define Next Steps.

B. Review the Team's Objective

The Team Leader provided team members with copies of the team's objective below which was crafted by the organization's Leadership Team.

The overall objective of the Meetings Transformation Team is to help make our meetings more effective, more efficient, and more productive.

C. Identify Critical Issues

Team members were asked to identify the key items that they felt needed to be addressed in order to ensure we achieved our objective. These items are listed below. The Team Leader indicated that, throughout the process, we will be coming back to this list and adding to it to ensure that all issues are covered.

o   Getting everyone on board.

o   Addressing managers who chronically lead bad meetings.

o   Avoiding starting with a bang and then fizzling out.

o   Determining how to measure our success.

o   Participating on this team while maintaining full work responsibilities.

o   Identifying when we are done.

D. Confirm the Team's Work Process

The Team Leader presented The Master Plan—a proposed work process. After a lengthy discussion during which modifications were made to the proposed process, the team agreed to the following work tasks:

o   Identify the problems we see in our meetings to provide a starting list of what needs to be fixed.

o   Conduct a meeting survey to document a baseline of how we are performing with meetings.

o   Finalize Your Meeting Rights, Our Meeting Vision, and The Master Plan.

o   Finalize measurable outcomes that will define success for the initiative.

o   Develop a support plan—including training, tutorials, and samples—to build up skills in those who lead or participate in meetings.

o   Develop our plan for rewards and accountability.

o   Develop our plan for monitoring progress and communicating results.

o   Present a draft to senior management for approval.

o   Refine recommendations based on senior management input.

o   Execute The Master Plan, including monitoring results.

E. Define Team Norms and Decision-making Method

The participants agreed to the following norms for the team:

o Everyone will participate.
o We will have one conversation in the room.
o We will fully participate in each meeting.
o We will leave cell phones, Blackberries, and computers off (except for the documenter).
o We will speak positively of the team and of each other.
o We will respect one another's time by arriving at least five minutes in advance for all meetings so that we can start on time.
o We will take personal responsibility to be prepared for each meeting by reading all materials in advance.
o We will speak up about any issues or concerns we have.
o We will use five-finger consensus for all major decisions.
o We will operate all meetings as <u>Masterful Meetings</u>.

F. Decide Logistics for Meetings

The participants agreed to the following parameters for our meetings:

o We will meet every other Thursday from 9:00 a.m. to 11:30 a.m. in Conference Room A.

G. Identify Existing Problems with Meetings

The team began its work process by identifying existing problems with meetings.

o No agenda.
o Minimal participation.
o Going off track.
o Side conversations.
o No decisions.
o No results.
o Sarcastic comments.
o Too many agenda items.
o No real purpose to meet.
o One person dominating.
o Too much detail.
o No follow-up.

H. Next Steps

The team will meet again on 7/26/xx from 9:00 a.m. to 11:30 a.m. Our focus will be on the following:

o   Review action list.

o   Define Step 2: Meeting Survey.

o   Define Step 3: Meeting Vision Components.

o   Discuss how to participate on the team and still get a full workload done. (This may entail a recommendation to the Leadership Team.)

I. Decisions List

The following is an ongoing list of decisions made by the team with the date that the decision was made.

1.   We agreed to team norms (7/12/xx).
2.   We agreed on our work process (7/12/xx).
3.   We will meet every other Thursday from 9:00 a.m. to 11:30 a.m. in Conference Room A (7/12/xx).

J. Actions List

The following is an ongoing list of actions to be taken outside of the meeting along with the due date and the person responsible. When an action is completed, it appears in the next meeting notes as "done" and is then removed from subsequent meeting notes.

1.   Document and distribute the meeting notes. (Bill G., 7/17/nn)
2.   Review the draft survey and the draft meeting vision components from the book, and come to the meeting with recommended changes. (All, 7/26/xx)

Summary: The Secrets to Closing and Follow-up

In summary, the secrets to closing *Masterful Meetings* and following-up effectively include the following:

Secret 23. Prior to closing the meeting, be sure to thoroughly review the following:
- The agenda and all items covered in the meeting and any key topics or participant outcomes identified at the start.
- The decisions made by the team, documenting benefits if necessary.
- Any open issues in order to determine what action, if any, is needed on them.
- All actions to ensure that a person and a date are assigned to each

Secret 24. Use a brief process of identifying strengths, improvements, and a rating for the meeting to gain valuable feedback on how to improve future meetings.

Secret 25. To maintain clarity around decisions made and actions to be taken as a result of the meeting, distribute a summary following the meeting that includes decisions, actions, open issues, and relevant analysis documented during the meeting.

Secret 26. To help ensure that actions assigned during the meeting are accomplished, distribute a notice highlighting actions to be completed prior to the next meeting several days before that meeting. Additionally, in the next meeting, include a review of prior actions as the first or second agenda item.

Part III.
What If?

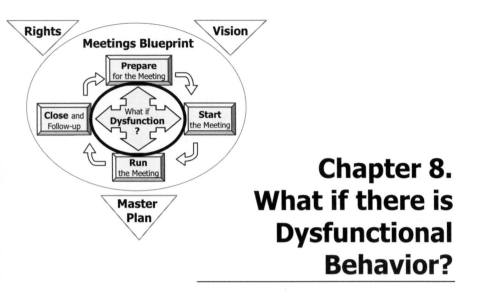

Chapter 8. What if there is Dysfunctional Behavior?

Introduction

What if, in the middle of the meeting, someone starts talking about something that is completely off topic? Or what if two people start whispering? Or what if someone verbally attacks one of the other meeting participants? This chapter focuses on some of the more common dysfunctional behaviors that happen in meetings.[10]

How should you respond to a dysfunction? Of course, this depends on the dysfunction and other factors, including when it occurs, the number of people affected, and the probable root cause. However, consider the following general formula:

General Formula for Addressing Dysfunction

❑ Approach privately or generally.
- Either speak with the people one-on-one during a break, or address the behaviors generally to the group without singling out any individuals. At times, however, singling out individuals during the meeting may be unavoidable.

❑ Empathize with the symptom.
- Praise an appropriate aspect of their behavior or express concern about the situation they find themselves in.

❑   Address the root cause.
-    Make an effort to get at the real issue by asking a question that will yield a response that confirms the issue.
❑   Get agreement on the solution.
-    Get agreement on how the situation will be handled going forward. Be sure that the solution addresses the root cause and not just the symptom.

With each of the common dysfunctions that follow, I have provided a description of the dysfunction, its likely causes, strategies to take to prevent the dysfunction, what to do "in the moment" when the dysfunction occurs, and what to do "after the moment" to further address the dysfunction. While most descriptions are for individual dysfunctions, the last two are for dysfunctions related to the entire group.

❑   Cell Phone Junkie
❑   Door Slammer
❑   Drop-out
❑   Interrupter
❑   Late Arriver/Early Leaver
❑   Loudmouth
❑   Naysayer
❑   Physical Attacker
❑   Storyteller
❑   Topic Jumper
❑   Verbal Attacker
❑   Whisperer
❑   Workaholic
❑   Group: Low Energy
❑   Group: Time Pressures

Study the various dysfunctions. Understand their common causes, the prevention strategies, and the actions to take in the moment. Advanced preparation can help you prevent dysfunction and respond appropriately should the need arise.

The Cell Phone Junkie

Description	The person's cell phone constantly rings, or the person is on and off the cell phone frequently.
Common Causes	❑ The person has a high priority activity that requires attention during the meeting. ❑ The person is unaware of how cell phone activity can reduce the effectiveness of the meeting for all participants. ❑ The person sees little value in the meeting and is attempting to make the best of having to be present.
Prevention	❑ Establish a ground rule: no cell phone calls during the meeting.
In the Moment	If a private conversation is possible: ❑ "It looks like people don't know you're in an important meeting, so they keep interrupting you. Have you been able to get the problem addressed? Is it okay then to turn the cell phone off for the rest of the meeting?" If a private conversation is *not* possible: ❑ "When I heard Tony's phone, it was a reminder to me that we need to keep cell phones off if we can. I want to check in with the group to make sure this won't be a problem."
After the Moment	❑ Discuss the issue privately to ensure that no additional problems exist.

The Door Slammer

Description	The person leaves the room in apparent disgust.
Common Causes	❏ The person has an issue unrelated to the meeting that needs immediate attention. ❏ The person does not believe the meeting is worth investing additional time. ❏ The person is dissatisfied with the meeting content or meeting process.
Prevention	❏ Establish a ground rule: everyone speaks about issues in the room; we will discuss the un-discussable.
In the Moment	❏ "Wow, Bill just got up and left the room. Given what felt like abruptness, I don't think it was because he had to go to the rest room." ❏ "We could try to continue working, but I bet many people are thinking about Bill's departure. So I would like to take a few minutes to get clarity on what just happened. Who can take a shot at explaining what happened and why you think it happened?" ❏ "So we have talked about what happened, and we have a guess as to why it may have happened. Now I have two other questions. What should we do about Bill? And what needs to happen differently to keep the rest of us from doing what Bill just did?" ❏ By taking a few minutes for debriefing, the group creates a common view of the incident.
After the Moment	❏ Follow-up to ensure that the agreed on actions are taken. Consider meeting privately with the person yourself.

The Drop-out

Description	The person does not participate in the discussion.
Common Causes	❑ The person has an introverted communication style and rarely offers comments in a group discussion. ❑ The person is typically talkative but is less involved in the discussion because of work pressures or other factors outside of the meeting. ❑ The person is dissatisfied with what is being discussed or the way the meeting is being run.
Prevention	❑ Establish a ground rule: everyone speaks.
In the Moment	❑ "Let's hear from everyone on this next point. With this question, I would like to start with [give the name of a person two seats to the right of the drop-out] and go around the room to her left. The question is . . ." ❑ A round-robin brain-storming activity such as this gets everyone involved. By starting two people before the drop-out, you avoid putting the person on the spot and you provide the person time to prepare an answer.
After the Moment	❑ Discuss the issue privately to ensure that no additional problems exist.

The Interrupter

Description	The person interrupts others or finishes their sentences.
Common Causes	❑ The person agrees with the comment being made, gets excited, and wants to show support. ❑ The person has little patience with the speed in which others speak. ❑ The person feels what they have to say is more important, or the person disagrees with the comment.
Prevention	❑ Establish a ground rule: have one conversation; respect the speaker.
In the Moment	❑ Interrupt the person. ❑ "It can be hard sometimes to avoid interrupting when you really want to say something, but we should stick to our ground rules. Can you hold that thought for a moment so that the person who was speaking has the opportunity to finish?"
After the Moment	❑ Discuss the issue privately to ensure that no additional problems exist.

The Late Arriver or Early Leaver

Description	The person habitually arrives late to the meeting or leaves early.
Common Causes	❏ The person has meetings or other commitments that make it difficult to arrive on time or stay for the entire meeting. ❏ The person does not believe the meeting is worth making full attendance a priority.
Prevention	❏ Distribute the meeting notice ahead of time. Indicate a gathering time of five to ten minutes prior to the start time. Indicate the importance of the purpose and products for the meeting. ❏ Contact the person in advance to gain commitment to be present for the entire meeting. Get agreement that the meeting should start on time with whomever is present.
In the Moment	❏ "I want to thank everyone for being here when you could get here and for continuing to do all you can to arrange your schedules so that we can start on time. Our next topic . . ."
After the Moment	❏ Discuss the issue privately to ensure that no additional problems exist.

The Loudmouth

Description	The person dominates the discussion.
Common Causes	❑ The person has an extroverted communication style and is not aware that a tendency to frequently speak first can limit the time and opportunity for others to speak. ❑ The person is aware of the tendency and needs help in balancing talking and listening time. ❑ The person intentionally wants to dominate in order to limit time spent discussing other views.
Prevention	❑ Establish a ground rule: have one conversation; share the air. ❑ Meet in advance to let the person know that you will be trying to get others to speak. - "I appreciate you being willing to speak, especially given that most have been pretty quiet. I need to get other people speaking more so that we can get their views on the table. So, during this next meeting, there will be times when you might hear me say, 'Nice point. Let's hear from some others on this.' This way, we'll get everyone's input."
In the Moment	❑ "Let's hear from everyone on this next point. With this question, I would like to start with [give the name of a person to the left of the loudmouth] and go around the room to his left. The question is . . ." ❑ A round-robin brain-storming activity such as this gets everyone involved. By directing the conversation away from the loudmouth, everyone else will be able to provide input first.
After the Moment	❑ Follow-up to ensure that no additional problems exist.

The Naysayer

Description	The person makes audible sighs of displeasure or negative statements such as "That won't work" without offering solutions.
Common Causes	❑ The person has a communication style that focuses on identifying problems and risks. ❑ The person opposes the idea suggested and is identifying reasons for the opposition. ❑ The person opposes the idea suggested and is attempting to create stumbling blocks to prevent adoption.
Prevention	❑ Establish ground rules: benefits first (i.e., give the strengths of an idea before identifying problems); take a stand (i.e., rather than describe what won't work, describe what will).
In the Moment	❑ Say with optimism, "You may be right. How do we make it better?" ❑ Naysayers often express their views negatively without offering alternatives. Avoid a debate about whether something is wrong by focusing their attention on creating something better.
After the Moment	❑ Seek to gain agreement to always state benefits before stating problems.

The Physical Attacker

Description	The person physically attacks someone.
Common Causes	❏ Disagreement during the meeting escalates into physical confrontation. ❏ Tensions or issues with a source outside the meeting escalate during the meeting into physical confrontation.
Prevention	❏ Identify probable issues prior to the meeting. ❏ Establish ground rules: discuss the undiscussable; be soft on people but hard on ideas. ❏ Actively keep the conversation focused on seeking solutions rather than assigning blame.
In the Moment	❏ Stop the meeting immediately. ❏ Let the group know they will be notified when the next meeting is scheduled. ❏ It is inappropriate to try to reschedule the meeting then since a physical attack can restart while the attempt to reschedule is going on.
After the Moment	❏ Consider meeting with the parties separately to identify the issues and an appropriate course of action.

The Storyteller

Description	The person likes to tell long-winded stories.
Common Causes	❑ The person has an extroverted communication style and is not aware of the tendency to be verbose. ❑ The person is aware of the tendency and needs help in getting to the point. ❑ The person is aware of the tendency and believes each story is worth the group's time and should be completely communicated.
Prevention	❑ Establish a ground rule: share the air. ❑ Meet in advance to let the person know that you will have limited discussion time in the meeting. - "I can readily see how stories give people a stronger picture of the point you are making. One of the concerns I have is that I've noticed sometimes people drop out when you begin a story. Is there a way that you can make your end point first and then shorten the story so that most will be able to follow? This may also mean that we can get to more things during our meeting. . . . So, during this next meeting, if I perceive that you may be starting a story, you might hear me say, 'Let's give the end point first so that people will be able to follow you better.'"
In the Moment	❑ "Let's remember the ground rule to give the end point first and keep it brief so that people will be able to follow along better."
After the Moment	❑ Follow-up to ensure that no additional problems exist.

The Topic Jumper

Description	The person frequently takes the group off topic.
Common Causes	❑ The person has a communication style that frequently shifts to a new topic before the prior one is complete.
Prevention	❑ Establish a ground rule: have one conversation; one topic at a time.
In the Moment	❑ "That's a good point. If it's okay, can we put that on the issues list to be discussed later and get back to talking about . . . ?"
After the Moment	❑ Consider seeking an agreement with the person to make an effort to use the issues list when new topics come up.

The Verbal Attacker

Description	The person makes a negative comment about or directed at someone.
Common Causes	❑ Disagreement during the meeting escalates into the verbal attack. ❑ Tensions or issues with a source outside the meeting escalate into a verbal attack during the meeting.
Prevention	❑ Identify probable issues prior to the meeting. ❑ Establish ground rules: discuss the un-discussable; be soft on people but hard on ideas. ❑ Actively keep the conversation focused on seeking solutions rather than assigning blame.
In the Moment	❑ Move between the people to cut-off the debate then slow down the discussion and reestablish order. ❑ "Let's take a time-out here. We have important issues to discuss, and we have established ground rules to help us do this. One of our ground rules is to be soft on people and hard on ideas. We will unlikely be successful if our focus is on blame or finger-pointing. I would like to continue the discussion, if we can, but only if we can do so respectfully and with an understanding of the problems and a focus on developing solutions. Can we do this?"
After the Moment	❑ Consider taking a break and reconvening the meeting later. ❑ Consider meeting with the parties separately to identify the issues and an appropriate course of action.

The Whisperer

Description	The person holds side conversations during the meeting.
Common Causes	❑ The person did not hear or understand a prior comment and asks someone for clarification. ❑ The person heard the prior comment and comments on it to someone. ❑ The person is having an unrelated discussion.
Prevention	❑ Establish a ground rule: one conversation.
In the Moment	❑ "Let's remember the ground rule that we want to have one conversation in the room so that we are respectful of the speaker and other listeners." ❑ Privately, if possible, give the "shhh" sign with one finger to your lips if the whispering continues.
After the Moment	❑ Discuss the issue privately to ensure that no additional problems exist.

The Workaholic

Description	The person does other work during the meeting.
Common Causes	❑ The person has a high-priority activity that requires attention during the meeting. ❑ The person sees little value in the meeting and is attempting to make the best of having to be present.
Prevention	❑ Establish a ground rule: meeting work only (i.e., work on only the meeting during the meeting).
In the Moment	If a private conversation is possible: ❑ "It looks like you have some important work to get done and this meeting has put you in a crunch. We do need your full attention if we can get it. Is this work something you can do later?" If a private conversation is *not* possible: ❑ "I know we established the ground rule of only doing meeting work during the meeting. I want to make sure that the ground rule will still work for everyone?"
After the Moment	❑ Discuss the issue privately to ensure that no additional problems exist.

Group: Low Energy

Description	Energy in the room is low.
Common Causes	❏ The group members generally have an introverted communication style and rarely offer comments in a group discussion. ❏ The topic is of low interest to the group, or the speaker or facilitator is presenting in a low energy style. ❏ The discussion is occurring during a low-energy period (e.g., right after lunch).
Prevention	❏ Ensure topics and speakers are appropriate for the audience. ❏ Plan the agenda to ensure that the group is highly engaged during low-energy periods. ❏ Have the group establish a simple recharge activity (e.g., "the wave") for use when the energy dips.
In the Moment	❏ "I'm sensing that the energy in the room is dipping pretty low. Let's quickly do our recharge activity to get the energy up." ❏ During low energy times, consider using round-robins in order to get everyone involved, (e.g., "Let's go around the room and get everyone's answer to this next question . . .")
After the Moment	❏ During the evaluation of the meeting, look for other possible reasons for the low energy, such as lack of interest in the topic.

Group: Time Pressures

Description	You are running out of time.
Common Causes	❑ The agenda was packed with too many items to cover in the time period. ❑ Too much time during the meeting was spent on items that were less important or off-topic.
Prevention	❑ While reviewing the agenda at the start of the meeting, establish target times for each agenda item. ❑ Put the items that are less critical near the end of the agenda. ❑ Use a timer to track time spent; alert the group when nearing the scheduled time for an item. ❑ Be flexible, allowing additional time when warranted and acceptable to the group but ending discussions when appropriate.
In the Moment	❑ "We have hit our time limit with this item. Can we end the discussion here, or do we need additional time? . . . Okay, let's give it an additional five minutes, but let's see if we can wrap it up even sooner." ❑ "It looks like that at the rate we are going we will not be able to spend the time we need to have a thoughtful discussion on the last agenda item. Does it make sense to move this one to our next meeting, or is another alternative more appropriate?"
After the Moment	❑ During the evaluation of the meeting, look for the causes of the overrun time. Identify knowledge to be gained about how much the group can tackle in a single meeting.

Summary: The Secrets to Managing Dysfunction

In summary, the secrets to managing dysfunction in *Masterful Meetings* include the following:

Secret 27. Understand the typical dysfunctions that can occur in meetings so that you will be prepared with prevention strategies and response strategies should the need arise.

Secret 28. In general, when responding to dysfunction:
  - Approach privately or generally.
  - Empathize with the symptom.
  - Address the root cause.
  - Get agreement on the solution.

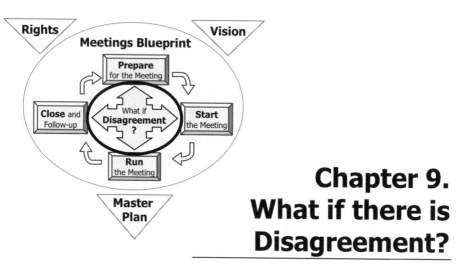

Chapter 9.
What if there is Disagreement?

When is a decision a decision? When do you have adequate agreement to move on? You should decide, or have the group decide, the method for decision-making.

Defining Agreement

What follows are several alternative methods for decision-making:

Leader Decides	The group will discuss the strengths and weaknesses of various alternatives, and the leader will make the final decision.
Leader Holds Veto Rights	The group will come to a decision based on one of the methods that follow, but the leader reserves the right to overrule.
Majority Rules	The decision is determined by the vote of a majority of the participants. Majority decision-making can be quick; however, it can also lead to less than optimal solutions and less than effective implementation because of limited discussion time and inadequate buy-in.
Super Majority	The group debates until a large majority of the participants agrees with one alternative. The super majority is often 60 percent, 67 percent, or 75 percent. However, supermajority can also lead to limited discussion and less buy-in.

| Full Consensus | Consensus encourages discussion until solutions are acceptable to everyone. While consensus increases buy-in, it can also result in watered-down solutions in order to gain full agreement. Additionally, consensus can take considerably more time. |

Five-Finger Consensus

As an alternative to the five decision-making methods above, I have found five-finger consensus to be far more helpful to groups. Here is how five-finger consensus works:

Steps in Five-Finger Consensus

❑ Once an alternative is proposed and discussed and the group is ready to check for agreement, the meeting leader explains that on the count of three, each person should hold up between one and five fingers indicating the level of support for the recommendation on the table.
   • 5—Strongly agree.
   • 4—Agree.
   • 3—Can see pluses and minuses, but willing to go along with the group.
   • 2—Disagree.
   • 1—Strongly disagree, and can't support.

❑ **In the first round, if everyone shows a five, four, or three, consensus has been reached**, and you can move ahead. If there are any ones or twos, those who indicate such are given the opportunity to explain why they gave the rating and make recommendations to change the alternative in order to make it acceptable to them. The originator of the alternative has the option to make changes or leave the option as it is and explains the decision to the rest of the group. Then the meeting leader tests five-finger consensus again. (If changes are made, it is a new first round.)

❑ **In the second round, if everyone shows a five, four, three, or two, the decision is made**, and you move ahead. If there are any ones, those who indicate such are given an additional opportunity to explain to the rest of the group why they gave the rating and make recommendations to change he alternative in order to make it acceptable to them. Once more, the originator of the alternative has the option to make changes or leave the option as it is and explains the decision to the rest of the group. (If changes are made, it is a new first round.)

❑ **In the final round, majority rules**. The decision is made based on a majority of the participants.

Five-finger consensus encourages the group to listen carefully when there is disagreement, and it encourages listening carefully twice, if necessary. And the technique doesn't allow a solution to be watered down because a few disagree.

The Three Reasons People Disagree

Disagreements generally occur for one of three reasons:[11]

❑ Level 1: Lack of shared information.

❑ Level 2: People have different values or experiences.

❑ Level 3: Outside factors are affecting the disagreement.

Let's look first at each of the three levels of disagreement and then at methods for resolving each one.

Level 1: Lack of Shared Information

In a level-1 disagreement, the people disagreeing have not clearly heard or understood each other's alternatives and the reasons for supporting them. Level-1 disagreements are often a result of an assumed understanding of what the other person is saying or meaning. Take a look at the sample below.

Sample Dialogue: Level-1 Disagreement

Pepper: I've been thinking about the problems we have been having with our performance review process, and I think I've come up with a solution: we should have our employees write their own reviews.

Michelle: Are you out of your mind? That can't work.

Pepper: Sure it can. You said yourself that most supervisors can't remember all the things their employees did in the prior year, and you said that last time, most of the reviews were superficial and based mostly on favoritism or on the last project people did. If employees write their own performance reviews, the focus will be on how people actually performed the entire year.

Michelle: No, I don't think so. Pepper, we have been partners for some time. But this has to be the craziest idea you have come up with in a while.

Pepper: I don't understand why you don't like it.

Michelle: Well, can you say, "Fox guarding the hen house"? If we let people write their own performance reviews, every review will be rated "far exceeds expectations." People won't admit their failures. Plus, this approach completely disempowers the managers. The performance review is an opportunity managers specifically have to influence the performance of their people. Letting employees rate themselves eliminates this. And what about—

Pepper: Hold on a second. I'm not sure you are hearing me. I said have the employees write their performance reviews, not determine their ratings. That's their manager's job. But if we have the employees write about their own accomplishments, strengths, and—

Michelle: And their areas for improvement. I get it. Then you have the manager review what the employee wrote and make additions and changes as needed with the employee in the room. Then the manager sets the rating. That makes sense. But why didn't you say that in the first place?

Pepper: I did say it. You just weren't listening. I said I wanted employees to write their performance reviews. What did you think I meant?

It's fairly evident what Michelle thought Pepper meant. When Pepper said, "We should have our employees write their own reviews," Michelle thought Pepper meant to have employees set their own ratings. Once Michelle understood what Pepper meant, they quickly realized they were in agreement.

Unfortunately, many level-1 disagreements are not resolved as quickly. People often argue without realizing that they actually agree. This condition occurs so frequently that there is a name for it: *violent agreement.* When a level-1 disagreement is resolved, you will often hear, "Oh, is that what you meant? Why didn't you say that?"

Level 2: Different Experiences or Values

In a level-2 disagreement, the parties have fully heard and understood one another's alternatives. However, they have had different experiences or hold different values that result in them preferring one alternative over another. The sample that follows describes what on the surface appears to be a level-2 disagreement.

Sample Dialogue: Level-2 Disagreement

Terry: If we are going to have any chance of transforming the meetings around here, we need to get everyone trained on what a great meeting is and how to create it. I understand there is a company that has courses on *Masterful Meetings*, and I think we need to get everyone in training as soon as possible.

Jordan: Everyone in training? Surely you're kidding. We can't train everyone in our organization. Maybe just the executives and managers. They are the ones who lead most meetings.

Terry: No, we can't limit this. It's not just the executives and managers who lead meetings. And just about everyone participates in one or more meetings every week. Everyone needs these skills. Everyone should take the course.

Jordan: When we do training, it has to be focused on the people who will get the most out of it. It never ceases to amaze me how you folks in HR want to get everybody involved in everything. You all need to keep in mind that this is a business. Training is an expense, not revenue, and it hurts revenue when you take people away from their real jobs.

Terry: Don't lecture me. I know about finances. The problem is that you guys in the field don't have a clue about what it means to empower people. If you took the time to make people feel like they are a part of the organization, you might be able to do something about your horrendous turnover problem.

This disagreement is going downhill fast. On the surface, it looks like a classic clash of perspectives, with the person in the field valuing operations and the human resources representative valuing people. We will come back to this disagreement later in the chapter.

Level 3: Outside Factors

A level-3 disagreement is based on personality, past history, or other outside factors that have nothing to do with the alternatives.

<u>Sample Dialogue: Level-3 Disagreement</u>

Sean: If our team is going to be successful with making major improvements to our performance review process, we should look at three to seven organizations known to do it well and identify their best practices.

Chris: That's a stupid idea. There is no way that will work.

Sean: Sure it will. We did something similar where I last worked. We just need to make sure we identify the right organizations.

Chris: No, It won't work.

Sean: I don't understand why you are being so difficult.

Chris: Because it won't work.

Leader: You may be right, Chris. It might not work. So what do we have to do to make it work?

Chris: There's nothing we can do. It just won't work.

Leader: Okay. . . . Well, how about explaining what's wrong with it?

Chris: Everything is wrong with it. It just won't work.

Leader: Help us understand, Chris. Why are you so convinced it won't work?

Chris: It just won't work. *He* thought of it. It won't work!

As you can likely detect from this example, the problem Chris has with the best practices idea doesn't seem to have much to do with the idea at all. Chris appears to believe that the problem is Sean, the person offering the idea. As it turns out, Chris learned some time ago that when he was interviewing to join the organization, Sean was one of the few people not in favor of hiring him. Since learning this information, Chris has felt any suggestion made by Sean couldn't possibly work.

Solving Level 3: Take it to a Higher Source

Level-3 disagreements are based on outside factors. Therefore, you can waste considerable time if you try to analyze the issue or identify alternatives because the disagreement does not concern either. To avoid wasting time on level-3 issues, recognize the signs:

Recognizing the Level-3 Signs

❏ Irrational arguments.

❏ No interest in considering or discussing alternatives.

How do you resolve a level-3 disagreement? Take it to a higher source. The following example uses the scenario from the earlier section featuring Chris and Sean:

1. Agree to disagree.	"Chris and Sean, can we agree that we are not going to agree on this point?"
2. Gain agreement to take it to a higher source.	"I would like to suggest the following: Let's the three of us go to the Vice President of Human Resources. Sean, explain what you want to do. Chris, you will have the opportunity to explain your concerns. And we'll let the VP decide what happens next."
3. Consider meeting privately to identify the core issue.	"I appreciate all the skills you bring to the team, especially when you are giving recommendations on how to fix things. I've noticed on a few occasions that you have disagreed strongly with suggestions from Sean. Tell me more about this. . . . Is there something I should do differently as the meeting leader? . . . Is there something up with you and Sean that may be getting in the way?"

Solving Level 1: Delineation

If the disagreement does not demonstrate level-3 signs (i.e., irrationality or no commitment to finding a solution), it is typically best to begin addressing the disagreement as if it were level 1: assume that all the key information is not necessarily known by all parties. Use techniques that slow down the conversation in order to encourage careful listening and comprehension. Consider the following steps:

1. Start with agreement.	"We seem to all agree that . . ."
2. Confirm the source of the disagreement.	"Where we seem to disagree is . . . Is that right?"
3. Identify the alternatives.	"So, Terry, you are saying . . . And, Sean, you are saying . . ."
4. Ask each party specific delineating questions.	"How would this work? How much? How long? Who is involved in . . . ? What is involved in . . . ?"
5. Summarize the information.	"Based on what Terry has said, this alternative will cost . . . And it will take . . . And, as a result, we will have . . . Based on what Sean has said . . ."
6. Take a consensus check.	"Based on what we have discussed thus far, how many would be in favor of . . . and how many in favor of . . ."

Delineation encourages each party to listen carefully to the other. When the disagreement is solely because of a lack of shared information, the parties quickly learn that they did not disagree at all. Either they did not hear each other, heard but did not understand each other, or did not share relevant information.

The sample dialogue that follows continues the disagreement between Terry and Jordan concerning who should take the meetings training. The dialogue picks up with Terry's last comment.

Sample Dialogue: Level-1 Disagreement Resolved

Terry: Don't lecture me. I know about finances. The problem is that you guys in the field don't have a clue about what it means to empower people. If you took the time to make people feel like they are a part of the organization, you might be able to do something about your horrendous turnover problem.

Leader: Let's slow down for a minute. It seems like you both agree that meeting training could help us, is that right?

Terry: Definitely.

Leader: Where you seem to disagree is on who should take the course?

Jordan: That's right.

Leader: So, Terry, you are saying that everyone should take the course.

Terry: That's right. (*Leader labels the first column "Everyone."*)

Leader: And, Jordan, you are saying something different?

Jordan: Yes, I think only key managers should take the class. (*Leader labels the second column "Key Managers."*)

Leader: Terry, you said everyone would take the meetings course. How would it work? How many people is that?

Terry: All six hundred of our employees.

Leader: Would each one take the full two-day course?

Terry: No. I would want the vendor to create a special half-day class for our people so that they wouldn't have to spend so much time away from work.

Jordan: A half-day course? Why didn't you say that? I have no problem with that. We can make that work.

Disagreement resolved. In this case, Terry and Jordan were in "violent agreement." They were arguing because they had made assumptions about what the other had meant. Delineation solves this.

But what if Terry really meant a two-day course? The chart that follows provides a sample of what a meeting leader might record on a flip chart as a result of the delineation steps.

Results From Delineation

Everyone	Key Managers Only
600 people	100 people
Sign up by team	Execs select managers
2-day class	2-day class
20 people/class	20 people/class
32 classes	6 classes (one-makeup)
4 classes/month	2 classes/month
$9,000/class	$9,000/class
600 people	*100 people*
8 months	*3 months*
$288,000	*$54,000*

At this point, Sean and Terry understand one another's alternatives but are still in disagreement. In this case, you would conclude that this is not a level-1 disagreement and would begin using level-2 resolution strategies.

Solving Level 2: Strengths, Weaknesses, Merging

If consensus has not been reached through delineation, the disagreement may be level 2: different values or experience. Start by identifying the strengths and weaknesses of each alternative. If agreement is not reached, identify the key strengths and create an alternative that combines the key strengths.

1. Identify the strengths.	"Let's take a look at each alternative starting with the first one. What are the strengths of this alternative?"

2. Identify the weaknesses.	"Now that we have identified the strengths of each alternative, let's look at the weaknesses. What are the weaknesses of this first alternative?"
3. Take a consensus check.	"Based on these strengths and weaknesses, how many now would be in favor of . . . And how many in favor of . . ."
4. Identify key strengths.	"Let's look at each alternative and identify the one or two most important strengths."
5. Create one or more new alternatives.	"Is there an alternative that might combine these key strengths?"
6. Delineate the top alternative.	"Let's delineate this top alternative to ensure that we all understand. How much . . ."
7. Take a consensus check.	"Based on what we have discussed thus far, how many would be in favor of . . . ?"

When you ask people the strengths of an alternative, their responses typically represent the values they hold that result in them preferring their alternative over the other. For example, those who prefer the "everyone" alternative place greater value on common language and everyone benefiting. Those who prefer the "key managers only" alternative place greater value on saving dollars and limiting time away from work.

The merging process encourages the group to create an alternative that combines the key values of the participants. The chart that follows provides a sample of what a meeting leader might record on a flip chart using the merge process with the training course disagreement between Sean and Terry described previously.

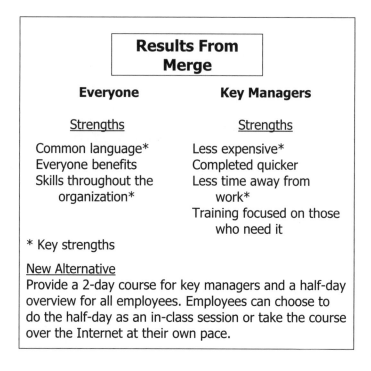

Summary: The Secrets to Gaining Agreement

In summary, the secrets to gaining agreement in *Masterful Meetings* include the following:

Secret 29. Use five-finger consensus as a decision-making vehicle to gain a broad base of agreement without jeopardizing the quality of a solution in order to achieve unanimous support.

Secret 30. When faced with a disagreement, determine whether the disagreement is level 1, 2, or 3.

Secret 31. Apply the appropriate consensus building strategy—delineation, strengths-weaknesses-merging, or higher source—depending on the level of the disagreement.

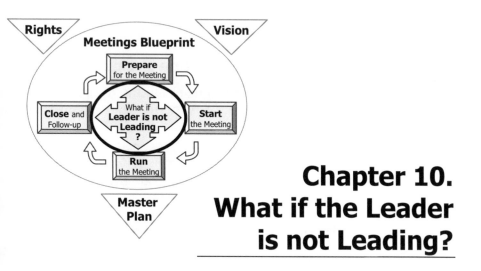

Chapter 10.
What if the Leader is not Leading?

There will be times when a meeting is not going well, but the meeting leader is not taking action. Rather than passively accept the bad meeting, *Masterful Meeting* participants can assist the leader by asking guiding questions that lead the group to take action. There are several situations in which guiding questions might be helpful.

The Meeting Starts without a Purpose or Agenda

If the meeting leader starts the meeting without stating the meeting's purpose or giving an agenda, a *Masterful Meeting* participant might say:

- ❑ "Excuse me. I may have missed it. Could you take a second to go over the overall purpose of this meeting, what we need to have when we are done, and your thoughts about the agenda? This will help me stay focused and make sure I don't go off on tangents. What's our overall purpose for this meeting?"

The Discussion is Getting Off Track

If the discussion seems to be getting off track, a *Masterful Meeting* participant might say:

- ❑ "These are excellent points we are discussing. I know we have to get back to our main topic, but I don't want to lose these points. Can we record them on an 'Issues List' or somewhere else so we can discuss them later and then get back to our main topic?"

Someone is Dominating or Someone Drops Out

If the meeting leader permits a person to dominate the discussion or if one or more people are not participating, a *Masterful Meeting* participant might say:

❑ "This is an important point we are discussing, and Joe has openly shared his views. It would be great to hear everyone else's opinions on this. Can we go around the room and have all of us give our views on this idea? I'll be glad to start . . ."

Decisions or Actions are not being Documented

If a decision is made or an action indicated and the meeting leader fails to record it, a *Masterful Meeting* participant might say:

❑ "It sounds like we just made an important decision. Can we have someone repeat it and the decision recorded so that we will have accurate documentation of what we decided?"

The Meeting is about to End without a Review

If a leader is about to end the meeting without a review, a *Masterful Meeting* participant might say:

❑ "After such a productive meeting, I would hate to leave without being clear on what we decided or what is going to happen next. Could we take a minute to review the decisions we've made and the actions that need to occur once we leave?"

Summary: The Secret to Guiding a Meeting

In summary, the secret to guiding a *Masterful Meeting* when you are not the meeting leader is the following:

Secret 32.   When a meeting is not going well and the meeting leader is not reacting, you can assist the leader by asking guiding questions that lead the group to take action.

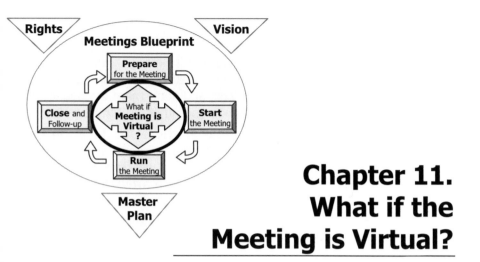

Chapter 11.
What if the
Meeting is Virtual?

How do you manage a meeting in which some, if not all, of the participants are in different places around the globe. Whether through audio-conferencing, videoconferencing, or Web-conferencing, technology today makes it possible for "virtual" meetings in which participants are no longer face-to-face.

Leading a *Masterful Meeting* using technology presents an additional level of complexity for the meeting leader. Despite the geographic dispersion, the meeting leader must still find a way to get the participants excited from the very beginning, keep everyone engaged and focused on the objective, gather and document the critical information, build consensus, manage dysfunction, and close with a clear understanding of what was accomplished, the value of the accomplishment, and the steps to be taken once the meeting ends.

Consider the following tips for managing virtual meetings.[12]

Preparing for the Virtual Meeting

1. **Prior to the meeting, distribute the meeting notice** including purpose, products, agenda, ground rules, and any relevant handouts. If multiple time zones are included in the meeting, be sure to specify the time zone when informing participants of the start and end times.

2. In planning the meeting, **limit agenda items** so that the entire call can be completed in two hours or less. If necessary, break the meeting into several calls.

3. Consider having participants **do preliminary brainstorming and submit ideas prior** to the meeting. You can summarize these ideas into "brainstorm lists" and send them in advance to participants along with the agenda and other written materials.

4. Consider having **multiple people at the same location assemble for the meeting** in a conference room or some other suitable environment. Having as many as possible in the same room promotes teamwork and helps people avoid the temptation to multitask.

5. **Create a roll-call list** that shows the name and location of each person expected in the meeting.

Executing a Virtual Meeting

6. At the beginning of the meeting, **conduct a roll call**: ask all participants to state their names and locations. Try to address participants by name throughout the meeting to help people link names with voices.

7. In getting the meeting started, perform a traditional "**inform-excite-empower-engage.**"
   - Explain the purpose of the meeting.
   - Get the participants excited about participating by explaining the benefits they will see from a successful outcome.
   - Let them know the authority that has been given them.
   - Get them involved by asking a starting question that engages them in meaningful discussion that contributes to the work to be done.

8. **Add specific ground rules** to assist with "virtual meeting etiquette," such as the following:
   - Announce yourself when joining the meeting, and inform the group if you are leaving prior to the end of the meeting.
   - Always identify yourself before speaking.
   - Avoid using the "hold" button, especially when music or other sounds result.

9. **Use round-robins frequently** to get input from everyone. Follow the same order each time, calling people by name. Establish this order early in the meeting.

10. **Establish a verbal method for doing consensus checks**, such as a round-robin, where each person indicates agreement or disagreement.

11. **Consider using meeting software** that allows all participants to view on a computer the information that is recorded while the meeting is ongoing.

12. **Do considerable summarizing** to make sure that everyone understands the focus of the discussion and what is being said.

Closing a Virtual Meeting

13. **Review all issues, decisions, and action items** prior to ending the meeting to help ensure full understanding and commitment to action.

14. **Publish a recap** immediately after the meeting.

Summary: The Secret to Virtual Meetings

In summary, the secret to executing a *Masterful Meeting* when there are participants who are remote includes the following:

Secret 33. When leading a meeting in which one or more participants are remote, establish special ground rules and use specific methods to maintain focus and keep everyone engaged.

Part IV.
Declare War on
Bad Meetings

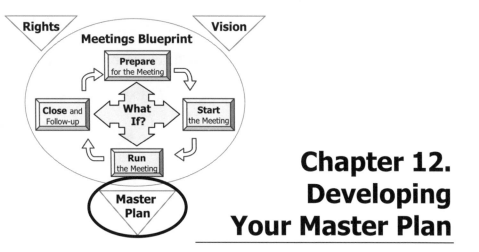

Chapter 12. Developing Your Master Plan

How do you do it? How do you ignite and sustain a revolution that raises the bar on meetings and rids your organization of bad meetings?

In this chapter, I lay out the activities that you can use as a starting point for your *Master Plan*. Review it. Change it. Make it yours. The sample *Master Plan* includes the steps we use at Leadership Strategies to help organizations systematically rid themselves of bad meetings. The steps start with your Leadership Team and include the creation of a Transformation Team. Over time, the revolution extends to every member of your organization.

As you create your own *Master Plan*, keep in mind the seven success factors that follow. Based on our experience, these factors can mean the difference between igniting a permanent transformation and sparking short-lived improvements only to have the organization revert back to familiar patterns of bad meetings.

Success Factors for Meetings Transformation

1. **Gain support** from your Leadership Team before taking any action.

2. **Establish a baseline** to demonstrate the need for improvement and to provide the starting point for determining if improvement occurs.

3. **Communicate a vision** of what a *Masterful Meeting* looks and feels like and what role meeting leaders and participants play in creating it.

4. **Empower every individual** to actively participate in eliminating bad meetings.

5. **Provide vehicles for improving skills** of meeting leaders and participants.

6. **Monitor and communicate progress** and take corrective action as needed.

7. **Reward** successes.

Sample *Master Plan*

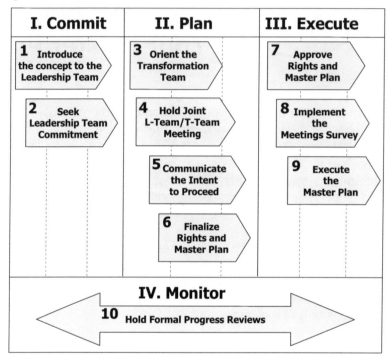

I. Commit	II. Plan	III. Execute
1 Introduce the concept to the Leadership Team	**3** Orient the Transformation Team	**7** Approve Rights and Master Plan
2 Seek Leadership Team Commitment	**4** Hold Joint L-Team/T-Team Meeting	**8** Implement the Meetings Survey
	5 Communicate the Intent to Proceed	**9** Execute the Master Plan
	6 Finalize Rights and Master Plan	

IV. Monitor

10 Hold Formal Progress Reviews

Step 1. Introduce the Concept to the Leadership Team.

For the revolution to be successful, every member of your Leadership Team must understand that bad meetings are hurting the organization and that a focused effort is needed to bring about change. They must understand that their role as leaders in the organization is to ignite a fire within their direct reports and to have their direct reports ignite a fire in their direct reports, and so on.

❑ At a regular meeting of your Leadership Team, and prior to handing out *Masterful Meetings* materials, let the Leadership Team know that you believe meetings in the organization need fixing.

❏ Describe bad meetings that you have witnessed and the negative effect they have had on the organization.

❏ Invite Leadership Team members to think about bad meetings that they have attended recently and to take a minute to tell their horror story. Consider asking the question this way:

> - "I'm sure I'm not the only one who has experienced bad meetings. How bad is it out there? I'd like to hear about some of the things you've seen recently happening in meetings. Think about the meetings you have attended in the last ninety days or so: the ones that were really bad. The one's that, for whatever reason, were ineffective, inefficient, or what have you. Let's just take a few minutes to hear about some of the problems we are seeing. Who can get me started?"

❏ Let them know that, as leaders in the organization, they are all responsible for either accepting bad meetings as the status quo or putting in place a mechanism for permanent change.

❏ Hand out copies of *The Secrets to Masterful Meetings*. During the meeting, have the Leadership Team take eight to ten minutes to read the first chapter.

- The goal is for Leadership Team members to gain an immediate overview of *Masterful Meetings* and the goal of eradicating bad meetings.
- At the same time, *Your Meeting Rights* may raise concerns about whether it makes sense to give everyone in the organization such rights.
- If Leadership Team members express this concern, let them know this topic will be discussed at the next meeting. But ask them to delay judgment until they have had the chance to review the entire book.

❏ Ask that each of them read the book before the next Leadership Team meeting.

- Get their agreement to come to the next meeting with specific ideas about whether the organization should undertake eliminating bad meetings.
- Ask them to come to the next meeting with their recommendations for modifying *Your Meeting Rights* and the *Master Plan*.

Step 2. Seek Leadership Team Commitment.

Hold a meeting of the Leadership Team to gain their commitment to proceed. Consider using the *Masterful Meeting* concepts in planning and running the meeting as a demonstration of a *Masterful Meeting* in action. A sample meeting notice follows.

Leadership Team Meeting
6/11/xx Gather 8:50 – End 10:30
Conference Room B

Meeting Purpose

To decide if the meetings transformation effort will be undertaken.

Expected Products

Go/no-go decision; and if "go," drafts of *Your Meeting Rights*, *Master Plan*, and transformation team assignments.

Proposed Agenda

8:50 Gather – 9:00 Start

A. Welcome, purpose, products, and agenda.
B. Likes and dislikes about *Masterful Meetings* concepts.
C. Recommendations for improvement.
D. Go / no-go decision.

If Go

E. Recommend preliminary modifications to *Your Meeting Rights*.
F. Recommend preliminary modifications to the *Master Plan*.
G. Identify meeting coaches for the Transformation Team.
H. Identify the executive sponsor.
I. Target a date for meeting with the Transformation Team.
J. Define next steps.

10:30 End

Invited Attendees: Leadership Team Members.

In Advance: Read *The Secrets to Masterful Meetings* and make notes on your likes, concerns, and recommended changes; identify potential meeting coaches from your team.

Bring to the Meeting: *The Secrets to Masterful Meetings* and your notes from your review.

The purpose of the Leadership Team meeting is to decide if the meetings transformation effort will be undertaken. If the team decides to proceed, they will need to customize *Your Meeting Rights* and the *Master Plan* to address the unique needs of your organization. Having the Leadership Team members customize these items will help to ensure that the meetings transformation has their buy-in and commitment to action.

The products of the meeting will be a go or no-go decision and, if a "go" decision is made, customized versions of *Your Meeting Rights* and the *Master Plan* with a Transformation Team named.

❑ Prior to the meeting, distribute a meeting notice based on the meeting-notice elements described in this book.

❑ Start the meeting with "thank you, inform, excite, empower."

❑ Next, review the agenda. You would typically engage next, but we will save the engagement for the very next step.

❑ To engage the Leadership Team members, ask them to give their opinions on the book and the transformation process recommended.

- Start first by asking team members to identify what they liked about what they read. Consider going around the room in a round-robin so that every person identifies at least one positive aspect.

- Next, ask team members to identify concerns.

❑ Ask team members to identify the things that they would recommend doing differently from what is in the book.

- You might ask the question this way:

- "Given these concerns, there are probably some things you would want us to do differently from what we see in the book. The book indicates specific rights and a specific Master Plan. What would we do differently? How would we make this work for us? If we were going to implement this revolution to eradicate bad meetings from our organization, what things would you suggest we do differently from what we see in the book?"

- Have someone record the comments on flip charts so that everyone can see and consider the suggestions. Consider using three flip charts labeled as follows:

Potential Changes to Rights	Potential Changes to Master Plan	Other Potential Changes

❑ As a team, decide whether to undertake the transformation.
  - To get the team ready to make a decision, you might ask:

> - "If we are going to undertake this transformation of meetings, we will need to discuss each of these potential changes in order to ensure that we are all in agreement. However, if we are not going to do this, there is no need to discuss the changes. This is where we make the decision. For this decision, let's agree that we will use the Five-Finger Consensus as described in the book. Recall that with Five-Finger Consensus, if you strongly agree that we should undertake this, give it a five; if you agree, give it a four; if you are on the fence but willing to go with the group, give it a three; if you disagree, give it a two; if you strongly disagree, give it a one. We will get a preliminary feeling first, and then we will go around the room and ask everyone to indicate why they voted the way they did. On the count of three, let's get a preliminary feeling from everyone by showing one to five fingers—five, strongly agree that we should invest in transforming our meetings; one, strongly disagree with investing in this. Is everyone ready? Okay, one-two-three. Show your fingers."

  - After an initial five-finger round, give all the members a chance to indicate why they voted the way they did.
  - After the preliminary discussion, if necessary, use a second and third round of five-finger consensus.

❑ Assuming that the group has agreed to move forward, develop a customized version of *Your Meeting Rights* and the *Master Plan* for your organization as needed.
  - Review each of the comments on the flip chart labeled "Proposed Changes to Rights." Decide as a group which changes to make.

- Review each of the comments on the flip chart labeled "Proposed Changes to Plan." Decide as a group which changes to make.
- Review each of the comments on the flip chart labeled "Other Proposed Changes." Decide as a group which changes to make.

❑ Have all members of the Leadership Team identify a meeting coach for their organizational units.
- The meeting coaches will coordinate the *Master Plan* within their area and will serve on the Transformation Team responsible for executing the *Master Plan*.
- Meeting coaches should expect to spend two to four hours a week in this role. More time may be needed in the beginning to get the meetings transformation firmly entrenched, and less time once the transformation moves into the monitoring phase.

❑ Assign one member of the Leadership Team to serve as the executive sponsor for overseeing the implementation of the *Master Plan*.
- The executive sponsor will serve as the principal leader for the meetings transformation and will head up the Transformation Team, which will consist of the executive sponsor and the meeting coaches.
- The executive sponsor will periodically report progress back to the Leadership Team.

❑ Decide the date for a joint meeting of the Leadership Team and the Transformation Team.
- This joint meeting will demonstrate to the meeting coaches the commitment of the entire Leadership Team to the meetings transformation.
- Likewise, during this meeting, the Leadership Team will hear firsthand feedback from the meeting coaches on the proposed *Your Meeting Rights*.

Step 3. Orient the Transformation Team.

The Transformation Team consists of the executive sponsor and the meeting coaches. The meeting coaches will need to understand the overall purpose of the transformation and the specific role they will play.

❑ Have the Leadership Team members meet individually with their meeting coaches to gain their commitment to help lead the transformation effort.

❑ Distribute a copy of this book to each of the meeting coaches, along with your organization's proposed *Meeting Rights* and the modified *Master Plan*.

❑ Ask the coaches to review the information and come to the next meeting with comments and ideas.

The Role of Meeting Coaches

Meeting coaches support the success factors for meetings transformation through the following activities:

❑ Serving on the Transformation Team.

❑ Developing the baseline to demonstrate the need for improvement.

❑ Communicating a vision of what a *Masterful Meeting* looks and feels like.

❑ Encouraging every individual in the organization to take part in eliminating bad meetings.

❑ Overseeing training and development programs for improving the meeting skills of meeting leaders and meeting participants.

❑ Monitoring progress and taking corrective action as needed.

❑ Communicating progress.

❑ Recommending rewards for successes.

Step 4. Hold a Joint Meeting of the L-Team and the T-Team.

The **purpose** of the joint meeting of the Leadership Team and the Transformation Team is to confirm the objectives of the transformation effort and the steps that will be taken. The desired **products** from the meeting are revised versions of *Your Meeting Rights* and the *Master Plan* and a preliminary schedule of events.

Leadership Team-Transformation Team Joint Meeting #1
6/25/xx Gather 8:50 – End 10:30
Conference Room B

Meeting Purpose
- ❑ Confirm the objectives of the transformation effort and the steps that will be taken.

Expected Products
- ❑ Revisions to *Your Meeting Rights* and the *Master Plan*; preliminary schedule of events.

Proposed Agenda

8:50 Gather – 9:00 Start

A. Welcome, Purpose, Products, and Agenda.

B. Meeting Coaches: Bad Meeting Experiences.

C. Meeting Coaches: Likes and Dislikes *Masterful Meetings* concept.

D. Meeting Coaches: Recommendations for Improvement.

E. Meeting Coaches: In Favor or Not In Favor of Proceeding.

F. Leadership Team: Review of Recommendations.

G. Roles of T-Team, L-Team, Executive Sponsor.

H. Timelines and Next Steps.

10:30 End

Invited Attendees: Leadership Team Members, Meeting Coaches.

In Advance: L-Team: Orient your coach. Coaches: Read *The Secrets to Masterful Meetings* and make notes on your likes, concerns, and recommended changes.

Bring to the Meeting: *The Secrets to Masterful Meetings* and your notes from your review.

During the meeting, take the following actions:

❑ Review the reasons that you believe the organization should ignite a revolution to improve meetings.

❑ Get views from the meeting coaches on the effect of bad meetings.

> - "Consider some of the bad meetings you have been in, the things that you have seen, and the things that have frustrated you. I would like to start with _____ and go around the room. I would like to hear examples of what you all have seen in meetings that you have attended: examples that demonstrate we need to fix this."

❑ Get views from meeting coaches on the information provided to them, using similar questions that the Leadership Team answered in the prior meeting.

- Start first by asking the coaches to identify what they liked about what they read. Consider going around the room in a round-robin so that every person identifies at least one positive aspect.
- Next, ask team members to identify concerns.
- After identifying likes and concerns, ask the meeting coaches to identify the things that they would recommend doing differently from what they found in the customized versions of *Your Meeting Rights* or the *Master Plan*.
- As before, have someone record these comments on flip charts so that everyone can see and consider the suggestions. Consider using three flip charts labeled as follows:

Potential Changes to Rights	Potential Changes to Master Plan	Other Potential Changes

❑ Determine the level of support from the meeting coaches.
- Ask the meeting coaches to indicate whether they are in fa-vor or not in favor of undertaking the transformation.
- If the meeting coaches are not in favor, it will be important for Leadership Team members to understand why and to identify, with the meeting coaches, the conditions that would have to be in place for the meeting coaches to be in favor.
- Discuss the comments and changes proposed by the meeting coaches.

❑ A final decision is not needed on the proposed changes at this time since the meeting coaches and the executive sponsor will be working on these details later. However, it will be helpful for the Leadership Team members to give their preliminary opinions on the changes.
- Consider introducing the comment segment in this way:

> - "The Transformation Team will be discussing the proposed changes at their next meeting. It would probably be helpful for them to hear input from the Leadership Team. So, as we quickly review each of the proposed changes, we'll take a minute or two for comments and indicate by a show of hands those for it, against it, and neutral. Let's get started with reading the first one and opening it up for comments."

- Record the voting for each one for later use by the Transfor-mation Team.

❑ Review the roles of the Transformation Team, the Leadership Team, and the executive sponsor.

Transformation Team
- Develops the *Master Plan* and *Your Meeting Rights*.
- Oversees the execution of the *Master Plan*, evaluates results, and recommends adjustments to the Leadership Team.
- Implements adjustments.
- Rewards successes.
- Reports quarterly progress to the organization.

Leadership Team
- Selects members of the Transformation Team.
- Reviews progress quarterly.
- Demonstrates support for the transformation.
- Models the *Masterful Meetings* concepts.

Executive Sponsor
- Leads the transformation effort and the Transformation Team.
- Ensures the transformation effort is achieving desired goals.
- Reports progress to the Leadership Team.

❏ Establish broad timelines and next steps.
- Determine a target timeframe for having the Transformation Team complete their planning and the final clean-up of *Your Meeting Rights* and the *Master Plan.*
- Set a date for a general communication announcing the transformation throughout the organization.
- Determine the timeframe for periodic reports by the Transformation Team to the Leadership Team.
- Establish regular meeting times for the Transformation Team.

Master Plan Broad Timeline	Target Date
1. Complete transformation planning and clean-up of *Your Meeting Rights* and the *Master Plan.*	
2. Distribute general communication announcing the transformation.	
3. Report back to the Leadership Team on progress. (frequency:_____)	
4. Hold first meeting of the Transformation Team.	

Step 5. Communicate the Intent to Proceed.

In most organizations, the informal communications network moves considerably faster than official communication mechanisms. Accordingly, an announcement about the work of the Transformation Team should be made relatively early to reduce rumors and inaccuracies about the purpose and work of the team.

❑ The announcement should cover the following key elements:
- - What are we doing?
- - Why are we doing it?
- - How? When? Where? Who?
- - How will we know we have been successful?
- - What are the immediate next steps?
- - What will be expected of each associate?

❑ The announcement should also alert the organization to the upcoming survey on meetings and the importance of collecting accurate baseline information on where we are today.

Step 6. Finalize *Your Meeting Rights* and the *Master Plan.*

The Transformation Team will likely require several half-day meetings to complete its planning work. The **purpose** of these meetings will be to finalize all components of the *Master Plan.* The **products** for these meetings will be updated versions of *Your Meeting Rights* and the *Master Plan.* Additionally, the team will develop the following components of the *Master Plan*:

❑ **Vision of a *Masterful Meeting*** defines a common view of how meetings in general should be planned, started, executed, and closed and provides meeting tools.
-   What are the different types of meetings, and how should we use each one?
-   What are the most important characteristics of *Masterful Meetings?*
-   What are examples of meeting notices, ground rules, meetings minutes, etc.?
-   What are the roles of participants and the meeting leader?

❑ **Meetings Survey** includes the questions that will be asked to all members of the organization to determine the current quality of meetings and specific problems. The survey will be repeated periodically to assess progress.

❑ **Measurable Outcomes** define three to six specific targets that will be used to assess progress in meetings transformation. The Transformation Team should recommend three-year targets as well as one-year milestones indicating progress. As a starting point, consider establishing one or two targets in each of the following areas:
-   Effectiveness: Are more of our meetings achieving their desired end? Are we getting better decisions?
-   Efficiency: Are we getting more done in meetings in less time?
-   Satisfaction: Are more people satisfied with meetings?

❑ **Support Plan** describes training, tutorials, coaching, samples, and other mechanisms available to help people improve their skills in leading and participating in meetings.
-   What will we provide for meeting leaders to improve their ability to run *Masterful Meetings* and to help ensure they respect the meeting rights of others?

- How will we ensure that meeting participants understand both their roles in meetings as well as their responsibilities for ridding the organization of bad meetings?
- What tools and aids will we make available for people?

❑ **Reward and Accountability Plan** supplies a mechanism for recognizing and rewarding meetings excellence and for identifying and addressing areas for improvement.
- How will we identify and reward those who excel?
- How will we tactfully address those who run meetings poorly?
- How will we hold ourselves and the organization accountable for improvement?

❑ **Communications and Monitoring Plans** define the steps for announcing the transformation and the vehicles for monitoring and communicating progress on an ongoing basis.
- How will we ensure that the meetings transformation is permanent?
- What process will we put in place to monitor and communicate progress?
- How will we decide on adjustments along the way?

❑ The *Master Plan* Timeline provides an overview of the major activities and anticipated timings for implementing meetings transformation. Using the broad timelines identified in the joint meeting as a starting point, the Transformation Team will establish additional dates for the major *Master Plan* activities. The example that follows gives a sample of the types of activities to be included in the *Master Plan* timeline. Your customized timeline may include fewer or additional activities.

Sample Master Plan Timeline	Target Date
1. Complete clean-up of *Your Meeting Rights* and the *Master Plan* activities.	
2. Finalize the meetings survey, the *Masterful Meetings* vision, and *Masterful Meetings* tools (e.g., Role of Meeting Leaders, Sample Ground Rules).	
3. Define a roll-out plan indicating the schedule for introducing *Masterful Meetings* into the various levels of the organization (e.g., by department, by location, by business unit).	
4. Finalize a support plan with training options based on a person's primary involvement in meetings (e.g., four-day coach and facilitator training, two-day meeting leader training, half-day executive overview, half-day participant overview, two-hour Web-based awareness training).	
5. Develop the rewards and accountability plan indicating how successes will be celebrated—including the types of rewards, the qualifications, and the frequency—and how problems will be addressed.	
6. Develop a communication plan and a monitoring plan indicating how frequently various audiences will be updated on the status.	
7. Develop the *Master Plan* timeline by establishing dates for the *Master Plan* activities.	
8. Gain approval from the Leadership Team for all components of the *Master Plan*.	
9. Distribute a general communication announcing the transformation and meetings survey.	
10. Develop a report of survey results, including recommendations for measurable outcomes that define success after the first year and the third year.	
11. Gain approval from the Leadership Team for the measurable outcomes.	
12. Implement the roll-out plan, the communications plan, the development plan, the monitoring plan and the rewards plan.	

Step 7. Gain Approval of the *Master Plan.*

The **purpose** of the second joint meeting of the Leadership and Transformation Teams is to gain approval for the revised version of *Your Meeting Rights* and the various components of the *Master Plan.* The **products** resulting from the meeting will be a list of revisions to *Your Meeting Rights* and the components of the *Master Plan.*

❑ Prior to the meeting, the executive sponsor will distribute a meeting notice based on the meeting notice elements described in *Your Meeting Rights.*

❑ The executive sponsor will also distribute to the Leadership Team the revised *Your Meeting Rights* along with the revised *Master Plan* and each of its components as developed by the Transformation Team.

❑ During the meeting, the Leadership Team members will provide their comments on the strengths, concerns, and recommendations for improvement as done in prior meetings.

❑ Use the five-finger consensus or another consensus-building strategy to decide the recommendations to implement.

❑ Get agreement from the Leadership Team to proceed with the transformation timeline as modified during the meeting.

❑ Following the meeting, update as appropriate *Your Meeting Rights,* the *Master Plan,* and the various components to be used in the transformation.

Step 8. Implement the Meetings Survey.

The purpose of the meeting survey is to provide a baseline of the current state of meetings in the organization.

❑ The survey will answer questions such as:
  - How much time are we spending in meetings?
  - What percentage of our meetings do we consider productive and effective?
  - Overall, how satisfied are we with our meetings?
  - What are the common problems in our meetings?
  - What are strategies we should consider for improving meetings?

❑ A sample meetings survey follows.

Sample Meetings Survey

1. In your typical day, about what percentage of your time do you spend in scheduled or unscheduled meetings lasting at least 15 minutes?
2. Overall, on a 1 to 7 scale, with 7 as the highest rating, how would you rate your level of satisfaction with the meetings you attend?
3. A *Masterful Meeting* is well-prepared, well-executed, and results-oriented with a timely start, a decisive close, and a clear follow-up plan. For the meetings you attended in the last 90 days, what percentage met this general definition?
4. Over the past three months, have meetings in general:
   _ gotten better? _ stayed about the same? _ gotten worse?

Answer the following questions based on meetings you attended in the last 90 days.	Almost Always	Most Times	Some Times	Nearly Never			
	7	6	5	4	3	2	1

5. Participants knew the purpose and agenda for the meeting in advance.
6. Participants arrived on time for the meeting and stayed for the duration.
7. The right participants were at the meeting.
8. People arrived having completed necessary assignments.
9. All necessary information was available at the meeting.
10. The meeting started on time.
11. The meeting leader reviewed the purpose, desired products, and agenda at the start.
12. People talked and listened with respect.
13. People spoke openly and honestly.
14. Disagreement was handled constructively.
15. The discussion stayed focused and on topic.
16. Participants honored the ground rules throughout the meeting.
17. All participants were engaged in the meeting.
18. There was adequate discussion and debate prior to making decisions.
19. No one person dominated the discussion.
20. Prior to ending the meeting, all issues, decisions, and actions were reviewed.
21. The meeting ended on time or early.
22. The meeting produced a decision or valuable result.
23. The time spent in the meeting was productive.
24. Following the meeting, a summary was distributed to all participants.
25. A follow-up process was used to ensure all assigned actions were performed.
26. The meeting was necessary and could not have been handled effectively through e-mail or alternative methods.
27. What things should we do to improve our meetings?

Step 9. Execute the *Master Plan.*

The Transformation Team will execute the steps in the *Master Plan,* including implementing the following:

❏ The support plan.

❏ The reward and accountability plan.

❏ The communications and monitoring plan.

Step 10. Hold Formal Progress Reviews Quarterly.

The executive sponsor should formally report progress to the Leadership Team at least quarterly.

❏ Progress reports should include:
- Actual results against the measurable outcomes established.
- Major activities completed.
- Key issues to be addressed.
- Plans for the following quarter.

❏ Initially, the Transformation Team should continue to meet monthly to monitor progress and make adjustments along the way.

❏ Over time, the Transformation Team's meetings will occur before and following each Leadership Team update in order to prepare for the update and to take action based on any Leadership Team comments.

Summary: The Secrets to the *Master Plan*

The *Master Plan* is designed to help you achieve each of the success factors identified at the beginning of this chapter.

Secret 34.   By working with your Leadership Team in advance, you *will* gain the understanding and support of your Leadership Team before taking any action.

Secret 35.   Through the meeting survey, you *will* establish a baseline to demonstrate the need for improvement and to provide the starting point for determining if improvement occurs.

Secret 36.   Through the *Vision of a Masterful Meeting*, you *will* communicate a vision of what a *Masterful Meeting* looks and feels like.

Secret 37.   Through *Your Meeting Rights*, you *will* empower every individual in the organization to take part in eliminating bad meetings.

Secret 38.   Through the support plan, you *will* provide a vehicle for improving the meeting skills of meeting leaders and meeting participants.

Secret 39.   Through the monitoring and accountability plans, you *will* have a means for monitoring progress and taking corrective action as needed.

Secret 40.   Through the communication and reward plans, you *will* communicate progress and reward successes.

Epilogue

When I starting writing *The Secrets of Facilitation* in 1998, I was convinced that many people could benefit from the knowledge of what facilitators do to achieve better results through groups. My goal was to write a book that had enough depth for the professional facilitator, but used simple examples that anyone who occasionally led meetings would find helpful. Although the effort was valiant, the 300-page book that resulted is a bit daunting for the casual meeting leader.

My goal with *The Secrets to Masterful Meetings* was to create the book for everyone: clear, concise, and formatted in a way that made the information readily accessible. I hope this book has hit its mark.

I sincerely believe that we must create a new vision of what meetings should be. We must expect more from meetings and not allow our time and energy to be wasted by bad meetings. We must empower people to make bad meetings simply unacceptable.

The *Masterful Meetings* framework provides a roadmap to get there. By executing the *Master Plan*, organizations will likely see dramatic improvement in the quality of their meetings in three to six months. With consistent monitoring, communicating, rewarding, and accountability, bad meetings will become increasingly unacceptable in an organization's culture.

For the meetings you run, use the checklists for preparing, starting, executing, and closing the meeting. As appropriate, bring your book with you to meetings. Demonstrate the techniques regularly.

Everyone should be entitled to meeting rights. And every meeting should be a *masterful* one. But this won't happen on its own. Please share this work with others and continue the meetings revolution.

Here's to *Masterful Meetings* everywhere,

Michael Wilkinson
November 2005

About the Author

Michael Wilkinson is Managing Director of Leadership Strategies—The Facilitation Company, an organization that specializes in training in facilitation, consulting, leadership, and meeting skills. Leadership Strategies also provides professional facilitators to help organizations with strategic planning, issue resolution, focus groups, and a variety of other processes.

Michael is the author of *The Secrets of Facilitation* and founder of the National Facilitator Database. He serves on the board of the National Institute for Facilitation and was one of the first five Certified Professional Facilitators in North America. In recent years, he has been awarded the prestigious Certified Master Facilitator designation and named Facilitator of the Year for his achievements and contributions to the field.

He is a much sought-after facilitator, trainer, and speaker, nationally as well as internationally. He has completed international assignments in Bangkok, Brisbane, Glasgow, Hamburg, Hong Kong, London, Melbourne, Milan, Singapore, Sydney and Wellington. He has worked with hundreds of public and private sector organizations, including The Coca-Cola Company, KPMG Peat Marwick, the Centers for Disease Control, and the United Way of America.

Prior to his current post, he was a Senior Manager in Ernst & Young's Management Consulting Group. As an accomplished information technology consultant, he was selected by the Governor of his state to serve for two terms on the state's twelve-member Information Technology Policy Council.

Michael resides in Atlanta with his wife, Sherry, and their two children, Danielle and Gabrielle. He gets a thrill out of teaching and facilitating, is a passionate football fan, and recognizes God as his source.

Leadership Strategies
The Facilitation Company

www.leadstrat.com
800.824.2850

Assistance in Meetings Transformation

Clients frequently ask about our services to assist in implementing *Masterful Meetings*. I have provided brief descriptions below. See our website at www.leadstrat.com for additional information.

Customized Books

❑ Contact us to have a customized version of this book created for your employees—*The Secrets to Masterful Meetings at ABC*. Our writing and design teams can customize the content and cover to your specifications.

Consulting

❑ We provide consultants who guide organizations through the meetings transformation process. As needed, we serve as project managers, trainers, coaches, or technical advisors.

Training

❑ We provide training services related to meetings and facilitation.

The Effective Facilitator	4 days	For people who often lead groups and project teams.
Masterful Meetings	2 days	Basic and advanced skills for managers who spend most of their time in meetings.
The Masterful Meeting Primer	Half-day	Overview for executives and meeting participants.
	Online 2-4 hours	A Web-based class you can take on your own schedule.

References

[1] Michael Wilkinson, *The Secrets of Facilitation*, San Francisco: Jossey-Bass, 2004, p. 263.

[2] Ibid., 34.

[3] Ibid., 72.

[4] Adapted from The Skilled Facilitator: A Comprehensive Resource for Consultants, Facilitators, Managers, Trainers, and Coaches (New and Revised) by Roger Schwarz. San Francisco: Jossey-Bass, 2002.

[5] Ibid.

[6] Ibid.

[7] Michael Wilkinson, *The Secrets of Facilitation* (San Francisco: Jossey-Bass, 2004), 88.

[8] Ibid., 92.

[9] Ibid., 124.

[10] Ibid., 173.

[11] Ibid., 205.

[12] Ibid., 274.